I dedicate this book to my children and grandchildren –
anything is possible. Believe and you will achieve.
And Archie, thank you for believing in me.

Donna

Thanks to Donna, Archie and Roxy's Girls for trusting us
with your stories, your recipes and your dream.

Tin Shack Press

Published by Tin Shack Press
First edition published 2022
This edition published 2023
ISBN: 978-1-8381218-2-2

Text copyright © Donna MacCulloch 2022
Design & production: Susan Windram
Photographs copyright © Alan Windram,
except otter photographs, copyright Ewan Soutar
Print prepress by Augusta Kirkwood

A CIP catalogue record for this book is available from the British Library

Printed in Lithuania by BALTO

FSC
www.fsc.org

MIX
Paper from
responsible sources
FSC® C107574

Tin Shack Press

Email: mail@tinshackpress.co.uk
Website: www.tinshackpress.co.uk
Instagram:@tinshackpress
Twitter: @tinshackpress

Roxy's

Cake & Bake

Donna MacCulloch

Contents

Introduction

Where it all began...

I was born in London, an only child. My father was Irish, my mother from Weston-Super-Mare. I spent a great deal of my childhood in the West Country, growing up with allotments that produced various fruits and vegetables. Discovering rhubarb at the railway lines – I love rhubarb and when I cook with it, it takes me back to that experience! In those days children roamed free on many adventures.

I wasn't very clever at school. I was quiet and shy and very naive. I wasn't a popular child, which didn't bother me too much. I had wonderful parents who always supported and stood by me. I liked people, I liked the stories and their life experiences which they shared with me... So many stories. But more of those later.

In school they decided I should learn typing and secretarial work as they told me I'd not get into nursing, which is what I wanted to do. I sneaked into a sociology class once. I so enjoyed it and I seemed to understand it. The fifth lesson in, I was discovered and wasn't allowed to return.

When I left school I worked in a bakery in Clifton. I started off selling cakes behind the counter, then went on to making them. However, my love was to go into nursing and being told I couldn't didn't stop me from trying. Many applications were sent off and many rejections received.

During that time I got a job in a nursing home. A very posh one. I loved it. I loved the people. There was one lady there who had been injured in a riding accident and she liked things done in a certain way. She took a liking to me and I was one of the few members of staff who were allowed to touch her.

I was 17 when I went to Wales to do my nursing training, I qualified in 1979 as an enrolled psychiatric nurse and then later, while living in Oban, I studied and achieved my degree and then became a staff nurse – not bad, as I was told by my teachers I would never achieve this. I wonder what they would say now. I loved nursing and had many adventures. Adventures and life experiences teach us so many things, I think they make you strong.

Skipping to my next adventure...another dream was to have my own cafe. I was working for Caithness Glass at the time and the premises next to it was a shop unit, a new build that was up for grabs. The gentleman who had built the complex was a Mr Witherspoon. I knew him to have a pleasant chat with and to have a laugh with, so one day I gave him drawings and a plan of what I'd like to do with the unit – I wanted to open a 'Friends'-style cafe. Friends was a very popular TV programme at the time.

Well, I dressed myself up, arranged a proper meeting with him ... and he laughed at me. Said I was only a sales assistant and had no idea how to run a cafe. So I went back to hospital work, dreaming and searching for my own cafe, and eventually all my adventures led me here.

My idea for Roxy's was that it was a cafe for locals, and if we attracted tourists it would be a bonus. As we've always said, baking and food hold memories. I believe it's an important part of who we are as people. By creating an enjoyable experience, then it begins.

My husband Archie was in the Army Catering Corp and he has guided and supported me through all the highs and lows of owning and working in a cafe – the mistakes made, successes achieved, and put up with my crazy ideas. We work well together, a mixture of grounding and recklessness. Roxy's has always been a joint effort.

I had my eye on a premises for a while. The business was in decline and opening hours had reduced. It had once been a popular venue. I did some investigating and found the owner, or rather the person who was renting it. He was wanting out of the lease, so after discussions with him we drew up ideas and plans to propose to the landlord. When you are doing this sort of thing you have to be discreet. Luckily, the landlord went with our ideas and a deal was made.

Archie and I were about to take on the cafe – I had no experience, just a dream. Archie, with his background in the Catering Corp, believed in me. I remember him saying, 'It's not easy, don't think you will be able to sit around drinking coffee and chatting to people'.

The premises had to be gutted – walls and ceilings had to be replaced, it needed totally rewired. Typical DIY problems. Archie did a lot of the work with the help of his uncle Fred, which we were truly grateful for. We opened on 17 November 2007.

The inspiration for my baking comes from my mother and a field trip with the St John Ambulance when I was 10 years old. Our leader, who was a teacher, took us for afternoon tea to one of her friends, who was a home economics teacher. She had baked the most amazing amount of cakes I had ever seen – and I remember thinking, I wish I could do that.

We have three children, James, Jonathan and Roxanna, whom the café is named after. When my children were younger we used to bake together, especially at Christmas. Mince pies were always a hit and teaching my children to make pastry was a wonderful experience, just like my own mother did with me. Now, when the opportunity arises, I bake with my grandchildren, all six of them – Aimee, William, Kyra, Iona, Aiden, and Ruaridh.

My dear mother-in-law helped me bake in those early years, which was a great help, one that I needed. The learning curve was massive. Joys, tears, rows were all part of it. Building a reputation and a standing isn't easy and takes time. Staying up until the early hours writing menus before the day of opening was frantic – we laugh about it now.

Over the years of running Roxy's, I've had customers asking me for my recipes and telling me that if I had a book they would buy it. Well, finally, here it is! I hope you love it as much as I do.

Pastry
& tips

Shortcrust pastry

340g (12oz) plain flour
100g (3.5oz) cold lard, diced
100g (3.5oz) cold butter, diced
1/2tsp salt
1 egg
100ml of ice cold water

SWEET SHORTCRUST PASTRY
115g (4oz) caster sugar

You will need a good size of mixing bowl.

Sift the flour into the bowl, add the salt, then place the diced fats into the flour, tossing the small cubes ensuring they are well coated. Then rub the fat into the flour with your clean fingertips to a breadcrumb consistency.

Stir in caster sugar at this point if you are making sweet shortcrust pastry.

Make a dent in your mix and add the egg then drop a dash of water into the hole, gradually stir the ingredients using your finger tips until it begins to bind, add a little more water if the mixture is too crumbly.

Work into a soft, not sticky, ball of dough, leaving the sides of your bowl clean. Now you know it is ready.

Leave the pastry to relax for a while. I don't tend to put this in the fridge unless it is an extremely hot day. However I do wrap it in cling film or greaseproof paper to stop it forming a skin. About 5 minutes should be enough. Now roll out to your requirement.

When rolling out pastry ensure it is on a well-floured table and after each roll, lift the edges to stop the pastry contracting on itself. You can do this several times as long as you don't overwork the pastry. You will know if it is over worked – it becomes non-pliable and dense.

Hot water pastry

1 LARGE PIE OR 4–5 SMALL

450g plain flour
100g strong bread flour
1tsp salt
70g salted butter, diced (you can use unsalted if you prefer)
150g lard, diced
200ml water

Place both flours and salt in a large mixing bowl and rub in butter. Set aside

In saucepan, pour 200ml water, bring to the boil and then simmer. Place the lard into the water. Once it has dissolved, make a well in the flour and gently pour the liquid in and mix using a wooden spoon, bringing everything together. Once the dough is cool enough to handle, work it with your fingertips and form it into a ball.
Wrap the dough in clingfilm and rest for a few minutes – don't let it get cold as the dough needs to be warm to roll out and mould into your required shape. The pastry should feel greasy to the touch.

Shape the pastry into a disc 10–12cm in diameter for your filling and a larger piece into a disc 15–18 cm for your lid.

If you don't have a pie dish, just use an empty glass jar or dish to cut your round shape. The round discs should be smooth with no cracks, mould them into the baking dishes or jars then chill in fridge for an hour. To release the pastry, pour hot water into the jar.

Fill the pie casing with your chosen pie filling.

Place your pie lid on top and crimp the lid, then brush egg wash (see page 18) over the pie lid to finish off.

Bake at 180c for 30 minutes.

Tips

BAKING TIMES
✳ Always pre-heat the oven. Use the centre of the oven when baking if possible.
✳ All ovens are different so it is best to check your cakes while baking so you can regulate the oven heat and timing to suit you.

BLIND BAKING
This is when you pre-cook your pastry. Lightly grease and then dust your baking dish or tin with flour, shaking off any excess. Line the dish with the pastry and using a fork prick the base and the sides of the pastry all over.
You have two options now. One, cover the pastry with baking parchment and fill with baking beans (either dried beans such as kidney beans, or special ceramic beans you can buy in a cook shop). Chill the pastry for 10 minutes before placing in the oven. The second option is to bake without covering with beans, which I prefer. Make sure you chill first before baking.

BUTTER AND MARGARINE
I use salted butter for my baking, however the choice is yours, you can use unsalted. I also use a good quality margarine in my cakes unless otherwise stated in the recipe. I find it lighter and it does not require excessive whisking. It is best used at room temperature.

EGGS
We use medium or large sizes.

EGG WASH
One egg whisked with a touch of milk. Quantities may vary due to how much you intend to cover. This will give your pastry a golden glaze.

FROSTING
When making frosting, although we have given measurements, these may very. If you don't like cream cheese then just butter is fine. Make sure the butter is soft and gradually add the icing sugar, and vanilla extract, whisking longer and on a slower speed.

GOLDEN SYRUP/ TREACLE
When measuring these, I find it can be tricky – which is a bit of an understatement! So warming these sticking ingredients helps and I don't usually measure them, I tend to say GLUG, GLUG as I pour and stop the excess with my finger. It never fails!

GRAMS AND OUNCES
For some of the recipes I use ounces. These have been calculated separately – use one set of measurements only, as they are not exact equivalents.

MILK ALTERNATIVES
In most recipes you can replace full fat milk with either semi skimmed, oat, soya, or coconut.

MELTING CHOCOLATE
We melt our chocolate over a pan of simmering water, making sure the water does not get into the chocolate. Once the chocolate has nearly melted you can turn off the heat and leave to cool, stirring occasionally – any small lumps will soon disperse.

PASTRY
✳ Your fats should always be ice cold, likewise your water.
✳ A dash of water is probably about 50mls
✳ Rubbing your flours and fats using your fingertips is the best method to achieve the sand-like consistency.

However using a food processor will work too.

❋ Don't over work dough, by this I mean cutting and folding it up again and again, because this will produce a tough result and you want a light flaky texture.

❋ When rolling out your pastry lift the edges as you go as this allows the pastry to contract and expand.

❋ Shortcrust pastry is typically quite crumbly and flaky in texture as the pockets of fat make the flour rise when baked. As a contrast, hot water crust pastry is less flaky and more crisp as the fat is perfectly integrated with the rest of the ingredients. The hot water pastry is traditionally used for pork and game pies as it holds its shape well. I find it's great for steak pies or small picnic pies which you can put any left over filling in.

RECIPES

When starting a recipe, first measure out all the ingredients required. Read the recipe a couple of times so you can gather up the necessary utensils.

TESTING YOUR BAKING

Always test the thickest part of the sponge or loaf. I tend to use the bounce back method – if it doesn't feel springy and light leave it in the oven a little longer. This is a useful method for sponges. For loaves I have a long, thin knife I use as it doesn't leave too big a mark on the loaf. But a skewer will do the same job. Pop your knife or skewer into the centre of the loaf. If it comes out clean you know it is cooked.

Base mix
& toppings

Base mix

This base mix as I call it, is used for so many interesting recipes. I find it useful and manageable. I'm sure there are toppings that I can still invent for it. On these pages are a few I have already made, but please invent some of your own.

QUANTITY FOR RECIPE

12oz plain flour
250g cold butter, diced
4oz caster sugar

Preheat oven at 160C/Gas 4. Grease an oblong baking tin and line the bottom with baking parchment.

Place the flour, diced butter and caster sugar into a food processor and whizz on fast for a few seconds, until the ingredients have the consistency of fine sand.

Pour the mixture into the prepared baking tin. Gently and evenly spread the mixture – don't press it down, a little shake and tap should do.

Bake in the oven at 160C–180C, depending on your oven, for 15–20 minutes or until the base is lightly golden in colour. Set aside and leave to cool.

 Tip: If you want a smaller amount you can just use half the mixture, the rest you can store in a clean glass jar in the fridge. It should be fine for a week.

Caramel

Many a time I've taken my eye off this and I've burned the saucepan – what a nightmare to clean!

QUANTITY FOR RECIPE

75g muscovado sugar
125g salted butter
1 tin condensed milk

Put all the ingredients into a saucepan and stir continuously until cooked through, ensuring all lumps are dispersed.

Gently bring to the boil, stirring continuously, then simmer until mixture is of a thick consistency.

Leave to cool then spread over base mix.

Lemon curd

2 large lemons
100g caster sugar
50g butter
2 eggs, whisked
200ml water

Grate both lemon skins to remove the zest. Slice one of the lemons into a saucepan, add the zest and the 200ml of water and bring to the boil, then simmer until lemon is soft.

Drain off any liquid. What is left of the cooked lemon can be whizzed in the food processor and then placed in sieve, then strain the lemon through and set aside. Discard any pulp left in the sieve.

Place a glass bowl over a saucepan of simmering water and add the juice of the second lemon, caster sugar, butter, the whisked eggs and the rest of the cooked lemon that you passed through the sieve.

Now whisk vigorously until it thickens like custard. You can turn up the heat for a short while until it starts to thicken. Once it does, take off the heat and place in a clean, sterilized jar, or use as soon as its cooled.

Tip: Cooking the lemon may seem like more work, but it's worth the effort, especially if you like a bit of a tang to your lemon curd.

Swiss meringue buttercream

A number of the recipes in this book, including this Swiss meringue buttercream have been contributed by one of our bakers, Mikaela. She has been with Roxy's for just over a year, her passion, creativeness and baking abilities have been a wonderful addition to the Roxy's team. The joy of baking is an amazing experience and when you can share it, it gives great satisfaction. The excitement this creates to experiment and develop new ideas is what drives us.

9 egg whites
600g granulated sugar
500g unsalted butter
3tsp vanilla essence
1tsp salt

To make the Swiss meringue you will need a pot of water and a metal bowl that will sit nicely on top, covering all sides and not touching the top of the water to form your bain marie.

In the metal bowl place your egg whites and sugar and whisk over the boiling water until it reaches 72C, or is combined nicely and the sugar is dissolved. This process is cooking the eggs so they are safe to consume.

Once it has reached the correct temperature place in a stand mixer mixing bowl and whisk until you have firm peaks and the mixture is at room temp. (Once it has reached firm peaks you can place in the fridge to speed up the cooling process.) Once the mixture is at room temperature change the whisk to the beater attachment and beat for a few seconds to bring the mix together. Now add the butter, bit by bit, allowing the chunks to be incorporated in before adding the next one.

Once all the butter is incorporated add in the vanilla essence and then the salt. You may need to add more salt to taste. Beat until nice and thick and smooth. At this point you can add in any other flavouring or food colouring, to allow whichever cake you are decorating to taste and look its best.

Tip: If the buttercream splits just place your bowl over the bain marie and allow the sides to melt slightly, then while still over the bain marie, use a hand whisk to beat until it comes back together. If the buttercream is too runny, place back in the fridge and allow to cool for 20+ minutes and beat again until you get your desired consistency.

Our Cinderella story

At one of our work Christmas night parties at the Royal Hotel in Oban, all the girls were dressed up and extremely excited, even though it had been a very tough shift. Colline decided to take her 'crocks' (these are her work shoes) so she could put them on when her feet got sore!

After a few Highland swings round the dance floor and a few flowing Proseccos, we all went home happy and tired.

On the Monday morning back at work at Roxy's, Colline was missing a 'crock' or rather her 'glass slipper'. However the crock was saved and so were Colline's feet when, not quite Prince Charming, but a lovely porter came round from the Royal Hotel with the missing piece of footwear, presenting it to a very embarrassed Colline.

Sunrise in Kilchrenan

Baked
traybakes

Amaretto slice

250g mixed fruit
100g flaked almonds (50g are left to sprinkle on the top of the mixture before baking)
150ml Amaretto liqueur
100g glacé cherries
130g margarine
130g caster sugar
4 eggs
170g ground almonds
2tbsp Amaretto for filling
1 packet of ready-roll pastry or use the sweet shortcrust pastry recipe (see p16)
Icing sugar

Preheat oven at 180C/Gas 4. Grease and line the bottom of an oblong tin with baking parchment. Don't bother lining the tin with parchment if using ready-roll pastry, which has its own lining paper on it.

Place the mixed fruit into a bowl with the flaked almonds, glacé cherries and then add 150ml Amaretto liqueur. Cook in the microwave for three minutes on high. Give it a stir then put to one side to cool.

Roll out your pastry and lay in the baking tin. Prick the pastry all over with a fork and blind bake for 10–15 minutes. (See page 18 for tips on blind baking)

While this is in the oven you can start to make the filling.

Cream the margarine and caster sugar until light and fluffy then add the eggs. Don't worry if it curdles. Then add the ground almonds and 2tsp of Amaretto and mix for another few minutes.

Evenly spread the cooled mixed fruit over the cooked pastry, then, using a spatula, scrape round the bowl and pour the batter mix on top, covering as evenly as possible, then scatter the rest of the flaked almonds on top and bake for 25–30 minutes until lightly golden. Cut into slices once cool.

To finish off, dust with a light sprinkling of icing sugar.

Apple caramel

Our apple caramel cake is especially loved by so many of our customers – I usually make one a day! While messing around with new ideas for different cakes and traybakes, and as apples and caramel go so well together, I decided to put a flangipan on top of the layer of shortbread, caramel and apples. Getting the right amount of ingredients was a bit tricky. The first time I had too much topping, which overflowed all over my oven – not helpful when you're busy. However, a few tweaks and hey, presto!

BASE
250g salted butter
100g caster sugar
340g plain flour, sifted

CARAMEL
1 tin condensed milk
120g salted butter
75g dark muscovado sugar

TOPPING
1 tin of cooked apples
140g ground almonds
100g of margarine
100g of caster sugar
3 eggs
100g dark chocolate
1tsp vegetable oil

Preheat oven at 180C/Gas 4. Grease a traybake tin and line the bottom with baking parchment.

Make the base and leave to cool (see page 22). Make the caramel (see page 23) and pour onto the base. Set aside to cool.

In a freestanding mixer, place margarine and caster sugar in the bowl and mix until light and fluffy. Then add the eggs and mix again until everything is incorporated. Don't worry if it curdles. Scrape around the edges of the bowl before putting in the ground almonds, then mix again until all incorporated.

Arrange the apples over the caramel, then evenly pour the almond mixture over the apples. Don't worry if it doesn't cover all the apples. Bake for 25–30 minutes or until firm to the touch and lightly golden. Check that the mixture is firm as it may need a few minutes more.

Using a sharp knife, cut along the edges of the cake tin and cake then leave for 5 minutes before turning out onto a wire rack, bottom side up, then onto a shallow tray with the apple side up.

Melt the chocolate in a bowl over a pan of simmering hot water – be careful not to get water in the chocolate bowl. Mix in oil. Drizzle this mixture over the cake and leave to cool. Cut into slices.

This can be served hot or cold, with cream or scoop of ice cream.

Original chocolate brownie

Mr P is a lovely elderly gentleman who is very charming. One of my waitresses, even when she is nearly ready to close lets him in for his two glasses of milk and sandwich or cake, as he doesn't mind her hoovering and closing up as he reads his paper. On one occasion this gentleman almost gave her heart failure as she found him with his head on the table and his eyes closed. She thought he was dead and nearly went into a panic, until he suddenly sat up and looked at her, and said: "OMG, did you think I'd died?" He then chuckled and said, "I wouldn't do that to you!"

200g dark chocolate, roughly broken up
175g of salted butter
325g caster sugar
130g of plain flour, sifted
3 eggs
Icing sugar

Preheat oven at 180C/Gas 4. Grease a traybake tin and line the bottom with baking parchment.

Place the chocolate and butter in a heat-proof bowl over a simmering pan of water until the chocolate and butter are melted. Don't let the water touch the bottom of your glass dish or get into the bowl.

Take the bowl off the heat and add the caster sugar. Mix well.

Sift the flour and add to the bowl, mixing well, then add the eggs and mix again. Once all the ingredients are incorporated pour the mixture into your prepared tin.

Bake for 20 minutes. The top should look slightly flaky once cooked and feel soft to the touch.

Turn out onto a cooling rack and peel off the parchment paper, then turn from rack onto a flat tray, ensuring flaky side up. When cool dust with icing sugar.

Cut into 12 squares.

Chocolate orange double frosted brownie

60g chopped Chocolate
Orange (small chunks)
250g of butter
500g caster sugar
120g of plain flour, sifted
100g cocoa powder
5 eggs
1 orange zest
1tsp orange essence

FROSTING
100g butter, softened
100g cream cheese
1tbsp cocoa powder
1tsp orange essence
Icing sugar

Pre-heat the oven at 170c. Grease an oblong tin and line the bottom with baking parchment.

Using a freestanding mixer place into the bowl the eggs and caster sugar, whisk vigorously until mixture has doubled in size and is light and fluffy, then add the flour, cocoa powder, orange essence and zest. Gently incorporate all ingredients then pour in the melted butter and continue to mix.

Using a spatula, mix in the chopped Chocolate Orange, then pour the mixture into your prepared tin and bake for 25–30 minutes – the brownie should be soft to touch but cooked and the top will have a cracked appearance.

Leave in the tin until completely cold, turn out and decorate with frosting and sprinkles or more chopped chocolate orange. You can cut into slices first then place chocolate segments on top.

To make the frosting put all ingredients in a bowl and whisk until you get the consistency you require.

This brownie has a lovely rich texture. We have made so many twists to this – here are some other ones we have created:
ROCKY ROAD To make this just add marshmallows, Maltesers, currants and cherries at the point where you add the Chocolate Orange.
BLACK FOREST version add morello cherries, 2 tsps of kirsch, and chopped dark chocolate.
BISCOFF Add a small teaspoon of Biscoff on top of your mixture, don't worry it will sink in while baking.
SALTED CARAMEL (pictured). Add a small amount of caramel (see page 23) dotted around your mixture and then sprinkle sea salt flakes gently over the mixture.

Fruit slice

I use shop bought shortcrust pastry for this recipe, but you can make your own using the recipe in this book.

2 x 350g of shop bought
shortcrust or turn to p16
1 jar or 411g mincemeat
200g currants
1tbsp cinnamon
1tsp nutmeg
1tbsp mixed spice
1tbsp vanilla essence
4tbsp hot water

Preheat oven at 180C/Gas 4. Grease a large flat baking tray and line with baking parchment. Shop bought pastry should have its own baking parchment so you will not need to line the tin separately.

First mix all the fruit, spices, vanilla essence and water in a bowl and microwave for 2 minutes, then leave to cool after giving it a good mix with a spoon.

Once pastry as reached room temperature, lay out one sheet on the large flat baking tray. If making your own pastry, roll it out to 1 cm thick.

Spread the mixture on the pastry sheet, right to the edges. Top with the second sheet of pastry. Pat down and prick with a knife, then brush over with egg wash (see page 18). Sprinkle with icing sugar.

Bake in preheated oven for 25 minutes or until golden brown. Once cold slice into 12 slices, or as many as you want.

Coconut caramel slice

This is so simple, yet so very popular. My sister-in-law thinks this cake goes well with custard. We have customers who like it warmed up. The funny, or not so funny thing is, the waitresses often get asked for this when they are really busy, and I know the last thing they want to do when the kitchen is busy and they're being called to take out food to other customers, is to ask the kitchen to heat up this cake. It's a dilemma – do they upset the chef or the customer? It's always the chef! Either way, I seem to get the blame because I invented this cake.

Base Mix, see p22
Caramel, see p23

6–7 large eggs
350g desiccated coconut
150g caster sugar
200g blueberries (optional)

Preheat oven at 180C/Gas 4. Grease an oblong baking tin and line the bottom with baking parchment.

Make the base and set aside to cool while you make the caramel. Once the caramel is made, pour over the base and, again, set aside to cool.

Put the eggs, caster sugar and coconut in a freestanding mixer and whisk vigorously until everything is well incorporated. The texture should be soft and wet.

Spoon the coconut mixture on top of the caramel base, gently ensuring it completely covers the caramel. I then use a chopping motion with the side of the spoon to make line indents into the coconut, so it leaves a pattern. Bake for 30–40 minutes until golden and firm to the touch.

Cut round the edges between the tin and the cake then turn the cake out onto a wire rack upside down, then turn it onto a tray, right side up and leave to cool.

I have also made a variation of this called lemon and blackcurrant jam coconut slice. Instead of making caramel, you spread a jar of blackcurrant jam over the base, and add lemon zest from one lemon, plus 1 tbsp of lemon juice to the coconut mixture. You can also add blueberries, mixed into the coconut topping.

Cut into 12–15 slices once cold.

Mrs G

Mrs G was a little elderly lady who you wouldn't mess with! She had a heart of gold but spoke her mind, although I never heard her ever say anything bad about a person. As the saying goes, "if you can't say anything nice, don't say anything at all".

She enjoyed the Bakewell Tart and many other cakes, as long as it wasn't lemon. She had an aversion to lemons.

On one occasion when she visited us at the cafe, I remember her calling myself over and Stephanie – one of our waitresses who had been with us for some time, who was young and had the perfect greeting for customers when they were placing their orders; I use to say to all the new starts, "now that's how it's done".

So, she called us over, which we thought was strange. She was sitting in the library area at table 9 and she usually sat at table 16 with my mother-in-law. "Come closer," she said, "don't let anyone see".

Stephanie and I looked at each other, then out of her shopping bag came a huge menu from a new cafe that had opened up along the street. Well, our faces were priceless – this little old lady had nicked the competition's menu!

"I took this when they weren't looking," she said.

We fell about laughing. Bless her heart, she thought it would be useful. What a wonderful memory she gave us, and how we laughed with her.

I often talk about this tale with the other staff and it makes us smile. Unfortunately this lovely lady is no longer with us, but what an impression she left.

Glen Nant

Lime & coconut slice

227g margarine
227g caster sugar
50g desiccated coconut
4 eggs
28g ground almonds
255g of self-raising flour, sifted
Zest of two limes
2tbsp of lime cordial
2tbsp milk

FROSTING
Icing sugar
100g butter, softened
100g cream cheese
Lime zest
50g desiccated coconut

Preheat oven at 180C/Gas 4. Grease and traybake tin and line the bottom with baking parchment.

Using a freestanding mixer, place the margarine and caster sugar in the bowl and mix on high speed until light and fluffy. Add the eggs and mix again until these are incorporated. Add the ground almonds, self-raising flour, coconut, lime zest (leave about a teaspoon for the frosting), lime cordial and milk, and whisk again for about 30 seconds on high speed. It's important not to over whisk the eggs and dry ingredients as this could make the cake too heavy.

Pour into the traybake tin and bake for 25–30 minutes.

Once cool, make the frosting by mixing together the softenend butter, cream cheese, and icing sugar until light and fluffy. If you start by making a small amount and gradually add more, you can get the consistency you require – not too soft, but firm and light. Add the lime zest, lime juice and coconut and mix again. Once done, put the frosting in the fridge for 10 minutes before decorating your traybake.

Set aside some of the frosting for piping. I use a light green colouring to add a swirl, but you can use whatever colour you want.

Cut into 12 slices.

Iced bakewell tart

I worked at Roxy's for about 10 years and only left this year after having a family. It is very hard work but has always been full of laughs. When I was younger, Donna used to make me skive off school to come into work. Stealing Archie's tea was the highlight of my day! – **Stephanie**

BASE
1 sheet of shop bought shortcrust pastry (or see recipe, p16)

Half a jar of raspberry jam with seeds. This can be exchanged for lemon curd if you want to make a lemon bakewell.

TOPPING
4.5oz margarine
4.5oz caster sugar
4 eggs
6oz ground almonds
2tsp almond essence

Icing sugar to decorate.

You can add the zest of one lemon to the topping, rather than the almond essence, if you want to make a lemon bakewell.

Preheat oven at 180C/Gas 4. Using an oblong baking tin, simply unroll the pastry in its own greaseproof paper and place in the tin (or grease the tin and line with baking parchment before placing pastry in tin.)

Press the pastry down into the corners and along the edges at the top of the tin. Prick the pastry all over with a fork, then blind bake (see page 18) for around 10–15 minutes, until the pastry is lightly coloured. Leave to cool for 5 minutes then spread the raspberry jam over the pastry.

Using a freestanding mixer, whisk together the margarine and caster sugar until light and fluffy, then whisk in the eggs. Don't worry if it curdles. Whisk in the ground almonds and essence until well incorporated. Pour the filling onto the jam, covering completely.

Bake for 25–30 minutes or until golden. Leave to cool in the fridge, then remove from the tin and decorate.

Pour some icing sugar into a mixing bowl and gradually add some water, stirring vigorously until smooth and dropping off the spoon. Do this until you have enough to cover your bakewell tart. The mixture needs to be not too runny and not too stiff – I sound just like the three bears!

Spread evenly and gently using a pallet knife then set in the fridge – at least two hours, but overnight is best. Top with glacé cherries.

Paradise slice

BASE
12oz plain flour
4oz caster sugar
250g salted butter

TOPPING
110g margarine
150g caster sugar
4 eggs
150g desiccated coconut
75g ground almonds
1tsp baking powder
110g sultanas
Icing sugar
Jar of raspberry jam

Preheat oven at 180C/Gas 4. Grease and line a traybake tin with parchment paper.

To make the base place the flour, sugar and butter into a food processor and whizz until it resembles sand in texture. Turn this into the tin and evenly spread it – there is no need to pat into place as long as it is evenly spread in the tin. Bake in the oven for 15–20 minutes, then leave to cool. Once cool spread the jam over the base then set aside.

Now make the flangipan topping. Using a freestanding mixer, whisk together the margarine and caster sugar until light and fluffy, then add the eggs. Whisk again, then whisk in the ground almonds, coconut and baking powder. Once all incorporated, mix in the sultanas by hand and spread the mixture over the jam topped base. Bake in oven for 25–30 minutes.

This traybake can go brown and look baked, however you need to touch the middle gently. If it is very wobbly then leave for five more minutes. It may not feel completely firm, but it will be cooked through. If in doubt, test with a knife gently placed through the middle.

Slice round the edges between the tin and the cake with a knife and turn it out onto a cooling rack, then place right side up on a flat tray. Dust with icing sugar.

There is a variation I do with this recipe and I've called it lemon paradise (pictured). To make this version, replace the raspberry jam with a jar of lemon curd and replace the sultanas with mixed citrus peel. I also add the zest of a lemon.

We find this version is very popular in the café.

Oban Bay

Roxy's girls

We used to, and still do, call ourselves Roxy's Girls. For the Saturday girls who survive a season at Roxy's they deserve this title. It may seem daft to those who don't know, but until you have experienced working in a busy cafe, well, what can I say, it's not just hard work, it's full of laughter, tears and exhaustion.

I remember the times we have laughed uncontrollably because we would cry if we didn't. The buzz of the place, the speed that is expected from customers, the adrenaline rush, the fear a rush of customers brings, the eerie silence before the mayhem, of too many orders being made in the kitchen and the husband saying, slow it down! Hahaha! To the amount of hot drinks needing to be made and trying to get them out before or with the food. Finding tables for people waiting. And among all this is the waitress who suddenly finds she also has to make six deluxe hot chocolates and four milk shakes as well as coffees. Phew!

The tables that have to be cleared and cleaned ready for the next incoming'. The call of the bell from the kitchen and the call of the counter to take drinks out, you need concentration, skill, speed, politeness, friendly personality, and take time also to talk with the customer who is asking questions or needs assistance. When it runs well it is like a well-oiled wheel. The spills and drama of an order being wrong, the quickness to reassure and correct, the dark humour at times, trying to make light-hearted jokes and it not always hitting the right mark – "it's OK, it's my husband is in the kitchen, I'll just kill him later – if you see blood, it's all good!"

So the girls that survive this deserve a medal. They work extremely hard and care about making the customers' experience a good one. This is just as important to them as it is to us. Sometimes this doesn't happen and we all reflect on the good and poor experiences to see what we can do better next time. This is what we do at the end of a shift, we sit round a table and reflect, laugh, curse and share the busy day's trials with each other before leaving the shop. These girls deserve this recognition of being a Roxy's Girl.

Sponges

Apple caramel sponge cake

Recipe by Mikaela.

225g caster sugar
225g unsalted butter
4 whole eggs
225g self-raising flour
1tbsp whole milk
1tsp caramel essence
Tinned apples

CARAMEL
See page 23

Make the caramel. Place in a bowl and set aside.

Preheat the oven to 180C and grease and line with parchment paper two eight-inch round cake tins, or an oblong baking tin. Set aside. Drain the tinned apples and cut into chunks, then set aside.

In a mixing bowl, using a whisk attachment, mix the butter and sugar until light in colour. Add the eggs one at a time, followed by the milk and caramel essence. Add in the sifted flour and mix until smooth, making sure not to over whisk. Roughly fold through a handful of chopped apple and two large spoonfuls of the caramel allowing a marble-like consistency.

Pour into the ready lined cake tins and bake in the middle shelf in the oven for 30–35 minutes until sponge is fully cooked and the skewer comes out clean. Turn out onto a wire rack and allow to cool completely before building and decorating.

Use the Swiss meringue buttercream recipe on page 25 to build and decorate the cake. Before building add some caramel essence to the buttercream to flavour slightly.

Cut both sponge in half so you have four sponges. Place your first sponge on a cake board or plate and spread a nice thick layer of buttercream on top, followed by a thin layer of caramel and a small sprinkling of chopped apples. Add the second sponge and do the same until all the sponges are layered together. Finish by coating the top and sides in more buttercream and decorate as you please.

Coffee & walnut cake

225g caster sugar
225g margarine
4 eggs
125g finely chopped walnuts, or
put them in a food processor
225g self-raising flour
1tbsp of coffee essence such as
Camp coffee or 2tbsp of rich
instant coffee dissolved in 100ml
of hot water.
1tbsp milk
8–12 walnut halves for
decorating on top of the frosting

FROSTING
150g salted butter, softened (use
more if required)
150g cream cheese (use more if
required)
300g icing sugar
1tbsp Camp coffee

Preheat oven at 180C/Gas 4. Grease two 8-inch round tins and line the bottom with baking parchment.

Using a freestanding mixer with a whisk attachment, place all the ingredients – except the finely chopped walnuts, which can be sprinkled onto your mixture before placing in the oven – in the bowl and whisk vigorously until well incorporated. About 30 seconds, until the mixture is light and fluffy. Be careful not to over mix.

Fill the two tins, sprinkle on the chopped walnuts, and then bake for 20–25 minutes. Check that the cakes spring back if lightly pressed in the middle. If not, give them another couple of minutes. Once out of the oven leave to cool for a few minutes before turning out onto a wire cooling rack. Remove the baking parchment gently.

While the cakes are cooling, make the frosting.

Mix together the softened butter, cream cheese, coffee essence and icing sugar until light and fluffy. If you start by making a small amount and gradually add more of the three main ingredients you can get the consistency you require – not too soft, but firm and light.

Once done, put it in the fridge for 10 minutes before decorating your cake. Top the cake with the walnut halves.

Cut into 12 slices.

Chocolate cake

We had a full shop and a coach party of Italians arrived. All they wanted was espressos and chocolate cake, and they didn't want a table but wanted to stand around the counter, as they would in Italy. I think Clare and Stephanie were about to have heart attacks! I thought it gave Roxy's an extra buzz – I always find cafe culture in Europe so exhilarating.

This cake can be made in an oblong tin and cut into slices, or in three cake tins to give a three-tier cake, which once iced looks pretty impressive!

275g self-raising flour
175g caster sugar
3 heaped tbsp Golden Syrup
3 heaped tbsp cocoa powder
300ml milk
150ml vegetable oil
1tsp bicarbonate soda
1/2tsp vanilla essence
1/2tsp sea salt

FROSTING
125g salted butter, softened
125g cream cheese
1 heaped tbsp cocoa powder
1tsp vanilla essence
Icing sugar

Can be cut into 8–12 slices

Preheat oven at 180C/Gas 4. Grease an oblong baking tin or three round cake tins and then line the bottom with baking parchment.

Using a freestanding mixer, place all the cake ingredients into the bowl and mix together on high speed until completely incorporated then pour into your tins.

Bake for 20–25 minutes. If you are using the three tins, they will need less time in the oven, probably 15–20 minutes.

Turn out onto wire racks to cool. While the cake is cooling, make up your frosting.

Using a hand-mixer cream the butter and the cream cheese until thoroughly mixed, then gradually add the icing sugar and cocoa powder. The consistency you are looking for is light and fluffy. You may need more of the butter and cream cheese depending on the amount of cake you have to cover.

Once you have the consistency you're looking for put it in the fridge for 10 minutes before decorating your cake – be inventive, adding sweets or chocolate and sprinkles!

Carrot & honey cake

This recipe was given to me by a regular customer and it has been a very successful recipe for the cafe. I feel it is important to share recipes to keep them alive, as I see it. I had a customer once who wanted this cake made for her daughter's wedding as a second cake for guests. Apparently it went down a treat.

4 eggs
150g caster sugar
300ml rapeseed oil
300g wholemeal self-raising flour
1tsp bicarbonate of soda
1tsp salt
350g grated carrots
200g honey (This can be warmed in the microwave for 1 minute, but remember to remove the lid of the jar.)

FROSTING
Icing sugar
100g butter, softened
100g cream cheese
1/2tsp vanilla essence

Preheat oven at 180C/Gas 4. Grease a large loose-bottomed tin (spring form) and then line the bottom of the tin with baking parchment.

Whisk the eggs and caster sugar together using a freestanding mixer on high speed for 10 minutes until the mixture has doubled in size and is light and fluffy.

Then add the oil and mix again for a few seconds. Reduce the speed when adding the oil.

Then add the flour (using the reduced speed), bicarbonate of soda and salt. Mix until all ingredients are incorporated. Then stir the grated carrots into the mixture by hand. Once the carrots are completely incorporated, pour the mixture into your cake tin and bake for 60 minutes.

Take the cake out of the oven and prick the cake all over with a small knife and then pour the jar of warm honey all over the cake. Leave till cold then top the cake with the frosting.

To make the frosting, mix together the softened butter, cream cheese, vanilla essence and icing sugar until light and fluffy. If you start by making a small amount and gradually add more, you can get the consistency you require – not too soft, but firm and light. Once done, put the frosting in the fridge for 10 minutes before decorating your cake.

Oban with McCaig's Tower lit up

Cuppa chino cake

275g self-raising flour, sifted
175g caster sugar
3 heaped tbsp Golden Syrup
3 heaped tbsp cocoa powder
250ml milk
50g Camp or strong coffee
150ml vegetable oil
1/2tsp vanilla essence
1tsp bicarbonate soda
1/2tsp sea salt

FROSTING
2tbsp Camp or strong coffee
Icing sugar
100g butter, softened
100g cream cheese

Preheat oven at 180C/Gas 4. Grease two or three round cake tins and line the bottom with baking parchment.

Using a freestanding mixer put all the ingredients for the sponge into the bowl and using the whisk attachment mix on high speed until all are incorporated. Using a spatula, scrape around the bowl to make sure all the ingredients are completely mixed together.

Pour the mixture into your cake tins and bake on the middle shelf of the oven for 20–25 minutes. Touch the cake lightly to see if they spring back.

Turn the sponges out of the cake tins and leave to cool on a wire rack and then once cool, cover with frosting.

To make the frosting, mix together the softened butter, cream cheese, vanilla essence and icing sugar until light and fluffy. If you start by making a small amount and gradually add more, you can get the consistency you require – not too soft, but firm and light. Once done, put the frosting in the fridge for 10 minutes before decorating your cake.

Coffee & hazelnut cake

225g caster sugar
225g margarine
4 eggs
225g self-raising flour
2tbsp of coffee essence such as
Camp coffee or 2tbsp of rich
instant coffee dissolved in 100ml
of hot water.
1tbsp hazelnut flavouring
100g whole hazelnuts to decorate

FROSTING
Camp coffee (or see above for
alternative)
hazelnut flavouring
100g butter, softened
100g cream cheese
Icing sugar

Preheat oven at 180C/Gas 4. Grease two 8-inch round tins and line the bottom with baking parchment.

Using a freestanding mixer, place the margarine, eggs, caster sugar, self-raising flour, coffee essence and hazelnut flavouring in the bowl and whisk together until everything is well incorporated.

Divide the mixture evenly between the two tins and then bake for 20–30 minutes. Check that the cakes spring back if lightly pressed in the middle. If not, give them another couple of minutes. Once out of the oven leave to cool for a few minutes before turning out onto a wire cooling rack. Remove the baking parchment gently.

While your sponges are cooling, make the frosting. The quantities shown are to fill the middle of the cake. If you want to cover the top as well, you will need to adjust the ingredients accordingly.

Mix together the softened butter, cream cheese, coffee essence and hazelnut flavouring, gradually adding the icing sugar until you have a firm, but light and fluffy mix. If you start by making a small amount and gradually add more of the three main ingredients you can get the consistency you require. If it gets too firm, just add a bit more cream cheese. Put it in the fridge for 10 minutes before decorating your cake.

Once you have filled the middle and sandwiched your two cakes together with the frosting, your cake is ready to be decorated.

Make some icing to cover the top of the cake by mixing the icing sugar with coffee essence and hazelnut flavouring until it is a smooth sauce – you don't want this too runny as you want it to set. Sprinkle the whole hazelnuts over the top.

Carrot & walnut cake

175g dark muscovado sugar
280g plain flour
3 eggs
2 ripe bananas mashed
175ml sunflower oil
175g grated carrots
55g walnuts, chopped (plus
enough for topping
1/2tsp salt
1tsp bicarbonate of soda
2tsp baking powder

FROSTING
100g butter, softened
100g cream cheese
1/2tsp vanilla essence
Icing sugar

Preheat oven at 180C/Gas 4. Grease a large loose-bottomed tin (spring form) and then line the bottom of the tin with baking parchment.

Using a freestanding mixer, place the sugar, eggs, oil, flour, salt, bicarbonate of soda, baking powder and mashed bananas in the bowl and mix together until everything is well incorporated. Using a wooden spoon, stir in the carrots and chopped walnuts by hand, ensuring everything is well incorporated. Pour the mixture into the prepared cake tin.

Bake for 45–50 minutes. To ensure cake is cooked through, prick the centre with a knife. If it comes out clean, it's ready. Leave to cool before removing from the tin.

To make the frosting, mix together the softened butter, cream cheese, vanilla essence and icing sugar until light and fluffy. If you start by making a small amount and gradually add more, you can get the consistency you require – not too soft, but firm and light.

Once done, put the frosting in the fridge for 10 minutes before decorating your cake. For extra decoration you can place walnuts on top of the frosting.

Coffee sponge

A delightful lady from Mull would always come in to have this when on her weekly visit to Oban. The times she didn't come in we worried. That may sound strange to some people, I suppose, but when you build up a relationship with your customers, it's hard not to. Once, we hadn't seen her for several months and it turns out she had been ill. Her friend came in to tell us, so we gave her a few slices of the woman's favourite cake to take to her, and a card wishing her well. Once she had recovered, she came back and it was lovely to see her again.

225g margarine
225g caster sugar
4 eggs
30g ground almonds
225g self-raising flour
1tbsp coffee essence such as
Camp coffee or 1tbsp espresso
coffee (two large spoonfuls of
coffee in 20ml of hot water)
1tbsp milk

FROSTING
150g salted butter, softened
150g cream cheese
300g icing sugar
1tbsp coffee essence (see above)

Preheat oven at 180C/Gas 4. Grease an oblong baking tin and line the bottom with baking parchment.

Using a freestanding mixer, cream the margarine and caster sugar until light in colour and fluffy. You may need to scrape the sides of the mixer and continue to mix for a while.

Add the eggs and mix again. Don't worry if it looks like it is curdled. Add the ground almonds, flour, the coffee essence and the milk, then mix again, but not for too long as you want to keep the mixture aerated.

Once the ingredients are well mixed, pour into the tin and spread the mixture gently. No need to smooth or compact it down as long as it fills the tin right to the edges. You want this sponge to stay light and aerated.

Bake for 25–30 minutes or until golden and firm to the touch. Touch the centre gently and if it bounces back, it's ready.

Allow to cool for a few minutes then turn out onto a wire rack. Once cold you can decorate it with frosting and a dusting of cocoa powder.

Serves 12.

Roxy's Coffee & Teahouse, Oban

Ice cream cone cakes

Colline and Stephanie were always up to high jinx in the cafe. On one occasion Colline hid Stephanie's shoe and Stephanie had to walk round serving customers with only one shoe on until she eventually found it! Stephanie and Colline would also tie their aprons together and walk round the cafe attached to each other!

12 flat-bottomed ice cream cones
Half a jar of raspberry jam or half
a jar of caramel spread

225g margarine
225g caster sugar
4 eggs
225g self-raising flour
1tsp vanilla essence
2tbsp milk, full fat

FROSTING
150g butter, softened
100g cream cheese
300g icing sugar (you can add
more if needed)

TO DECORATE
12 chocolate flakes
Sprinkles

Preheat oven at 180C/Gas 4. I use a muffin tin to help keep the wafer cones upright. Prepare the muffin tin by simply placing the 12 cones into the tray. You will need a piping bag for the decoration.

Using a freestanding mixer place the margarine, caster sugar, eggs, self-raising flour, vanilla essence and milk into the bowl and whisk together vigorously for a minute until all the ingredients are incorporated. Your mixture should look light and fluffy. Be careful not to over mix.

Put a spoonful of mixture in each cone then add a spoonful of jam or caramel. Top up with more sponge mixture, just make sure you leave about half an inch/2.5cm for the cake to rise.

Place in the oven carefully and bake for 20–25 minutes or until lightly golden in colour and the sponge springs back when touched.

Make the frosting by mixing together the softened butter, cream cheese, and icing sugar until light and fluffy. If you start by making a small amount and gradually add more of the three ingredients you can get the consistency you require – not too soft, but firm and light. Once done, put it in the fridge for 10 minutes before placing in the piping bag.

Once the cakes are completely cooled you can pipe on the topping using a spiral or rose petal nozzle on the piping bag, so it resembles an ice cream. Then pop a flake in and add some sprinkles on top.

Lemon & blueberry slice

This is a recipe that can have so many takes, I still find myself trying different flavourings – some work and some don't! Most of these recipes I had never written down, they were just in my head, but once you know a recipe you can tweak it and play around with it, inventing new methods and ingredients for it.

225g margarine (room temp not straight from the fridge)
225g caster sugar
4 eggs
225g self-raising flour, sifted
30g ground almonds
250g blueberries
2 lemons, juice and zest

Preheat oven at 180C/Gas 4. Grease an oblong baking tin and line the bottom with baking parchment.

In a freestanding mixer, whisk the margarine and caster sugar together until light and fluffy, then add the eggs. Mix again. Add the flour and ground almonds, the zest of the two lemons and most of the juice of one lemon – leave around a teaspoon of juice for the topping.

Mix again until all the ingredients are well incorporated – using a spatula scrape round the bowl before pouring into the baking tin. Sprinkle the blueberries over the top. Don't worry, they will sink a little bit.

Bake for 20–30 minutes until lightly golden in colour. If it bounces back when touched it is ready. Allow to cool for a couple of minutes then turn out onto a wire rack and leave to cool completely.

Mix the lemon juice and icing sugar together to make a thin drizzle icing, and once the cake is cold you can then drizzle the icing on top then cut the cake into slices.

Variations of this is to top with a lemon frosting instead then sprinkle more blueberries on top (pictured). Chill in the fridge for 5 minutes then cut into slices.

Lemon & blueberry sponge

There was this one chap who would come in a couple of times a week – the blueberry and lemon curd sponge was the attraction! He would discuss day-to-day things with you, but was quite quiet and seemed very mysterious.
The girls use to think he was a spy…some imagination they had! In time we found out that he worked for the railway and, at the time, he was sitting his exams to become a train driver. When he qualified he got a post to Mallaig. We made him his favourite cake as a leaving gift as we wouldn't see him again. We used to jest that we'd all turn up on his train, but, sadly, we never did. On one occasion we had a visit from some of his colleagues ordering his favourite cake as a birthday treat. Our cake was going to Mallaig!

225g margarine
225g caster sugar
4 eggs
225g self-raising flour
2 lemons, the juice and zest
250g blueberries
1tbsp milk
1 jar of lemon curd

FROSTING
150g salted butter, softened
150g cream cheese
300g icing sugar
Lemon juice from the second
lemon

Preheat oven at 180C/Gas 4. Grease two 8-inch round tins and line the bottom with baking parchment.

Using a freestanding mixer put the margarine, sugar, eggs, self-raising flour, the juice and lemon zest from one lemon, and teaspoon of milk into the bowl and mix together on high speed for about a minute until everything is incorporated, and has a light and fluffy texture. Then, using a spatula, gently stir in the blueberries while scraping around the bowl to ensure everything is incorporated. Save a few blueberries for decoration.

Divide the mixture between the cake tins and bake for 25–30 minutes until lightly golden in colour. The sponges should bounce back when touched. Allow to cool for a couple of minutes then turn out onto a wire rack and leave to cool completely.

For the frosting, cream together the butter, cream cheese, icing sugar, then add the lemon juice. You may need more or less of the icing sugar to get the consistency you want – the frosting should be firm but soft. Place in the fridge for 10 minutes before decorating the cake.

Once the sponges have cooled, sandwich them together using the lemon curd, then cover the cake in frosting, or just put it on the top if you prefer. Sprinkle the remaining blueberries and a bit of lemon zest on the top and add a dusting of icing sugar.

Pineapple & rum cake

250g plain flour
50g self-raising flour
1/2tsp of bicarbonate of soda
250g butter, diced
200g muscovado sugar
440g tin of crushed pineapple
1kg mixed fruit
4 eggs
2tbsp orange marmalade
2tbsp extra dark rum

Preheat oven at 180C/Gas 4. Grease a large loose-bottomed tin (spring form), or oblong, tin and then line the bottom and the sides with baking parchment.

In a saucepan place the pineapple, fruit, butter, sugar, marmalade and rum, and stir until well until everything is dissolved and combined. Gently bring to the boil then take off the heat and allow to cool.

Add the eggs and dry ingredients then mix with a wooden spoon until everything is completely incorporated. Pour the mixture into the prepared tin.

Bake for two hours. You may need to cover the top with tinfoil half way through baking to prevent the cake from burning.

Red velvet cake

380g self-raising flour
1tsp bicarbonate of soda
2tbsp cocoa powder
1/2tsp salt
115g margarine
400g caster sugar
240g vegetable oil
4 large eggs
1tbsp vanilla extract or
essence
1tsp white wine vinegar
240ml butter milk
3–4 drops of red food
colouring

FROSTING
250g salted butter, softened
250g cream cheese
1tsp vanilla essence
600g icing sugar, may need
more or less
If you prefer use the Swiss
meringue buttercream recipe
on p25

Preheat oven at 180C/Gas 4. Grease three 8-inch Victoria sponge sandwich tins and line the bottoms with parchment paper.

Using a freestanding mixer and a large bowl (the quantities for this cake are quite large), whisk the margarine and caster sugar together until light and fluffy. Then separate the eggs and add the yolks to the mixture, setting aside the whites in a separate bowl. Add the vegetable oil, vanilla essence and vinegar. Whisk again until everything is incorporated. You may need to use a spatula to scrape down the sides of the bowl to ensure this.

Add the flour and cocoa powder, bicarbonate of soda, salt and mix on a low speed. While this is mixing, gradually pour in the butter milk and food colouring – the depth of colour will depend on whether you are using liquid or gel. If a small tube of gel, you may need the whole tube. As you are mixing, if you feel it is not red enough, add more. Make sure everything is well incorporated.

Vigorously whisk the four egg whites in a separate bowl until they are fluffy and form peaks, then gently fold into the cake mixture using your spatula.

Divide the mixture evenly between the three tins and bake for 25–35 minutes, until the tops of the cakes bounce back when pressed gently in the centre. Leave in the tins to cool.

Mix together the softened butter, cream cheese, vanilla essence and icing sugar until light and fluffy. If you start by making a small amount and gradually add more of the three main ingredients you can get the consistency you require – not too soft, but firm and light. Once done, put it in the fridge for 10 minutes before decorating your cake.

Tip: When assembling the cakes you can gently slice a bit off the top of a couple, which, when finely crumbled, can be used to decorate the cake.

Sachertorte

This torte as many know is renowned, invented by Franz Sacher an Austrian who was only 16 when he made this. I would say it is a rich dark dense chocolate cake, best served with a dollop of cream and a really good espresso. I have made this occasionally out of pure enjoyment and, funnily enough, its history has several lucky twists of fate, similar to my own! I admire that.

130g dark chocolate (at least 60% cocoa)
1 vanilla pod
150g salted butter, softened
100g icing sugar
6 eggs
100g caster sugar
140g plain flour

200g apricot jam
200g caster sugar
150g dark chocolate (at least 60%) coarsely chopped
125ml water

Preheat oven at 160C/Gas 3. Grease a spring-form tin and line the bottom with baking parchment.

Place the 130g of dark chocolate in a glass bowl over a saucepan of simmering water and melt. Don't allow the water to touch the bowl. Once melted allow the chocolate to cool.

Using a hand-held mixer, mix the butter, icing sugar and vanilla seeds (slice the pod down the middle and scrape the seeds out into the bowl) until the mixture is light and fluffy and bubbles appear. Separate the eggs whites from the yolk and whisk the yokes into the mixture one by one, then gradually add the melted chocolate.

In a separate bowl, whisk the egg whites until stiff. Place the egg whites in the bowl on top of the cake mixture, then sift the flour on top. Fold everything together until well incorporated but aerated.

Bake in the middle of the oven for 10–15 minutes with the oven door slightly open. Then bake it for another 35–45 minutes with the door closed. The cake is ready when it bounces back slightly to the touch.

Loosen the sides of the spring-form tin and carefully slide the cake out onto a cooling rack. After 20 minutes pull off the baking parchment and let the cake cool completely.

Once cool, slice the cake horizontally, melt the jam and brush both cut sides of the cake with the jam, then place together. Brush the sides of the cake with jam too.

To make the glaze, put the caster sugar in a saucepan with 125ml of

water and boil over a high heat for five minutes. Take off the heat and allow to cool a little, then add the 150g of coarsely chopped chocolate. Stir until it forms a thick liquid, then pour the glaze over the top of the cake. Leave this to set for about two hours.

This cake is best served with whipped cream and a strong espresso.

Salted caramel cake

225g margarine
225g caster sugar
4 eggs
225g self-raising flour
30g ground almonds
2tsp salted caramel flavouring
2tbsp milk

FROSTING
Icing sugar
2tsp salted caramel flavouring
150g salted butter, softened
150g cream cheese

Preheat oven at 180C/Gas 4. Grease an oblong baking tin and line the bottom with baking parchment.

In a freestanding mixer, whisk the margarine and caster sugar together until light and fluffy, then add the eggs. Mix again, then add the flour and ground almonds, salted caramel flavouring and milk. Mix again until all the ingredients are well incorporated and then pour out into the baking tin.

Bake for 20–30 minutes until lightly golden in colour and the cake springs back to touch. Allow to cool for a few minutes, then turn out onto a wire rack and leave to cool completely.

To make the frosting, soften the butter and add the cream cheese and icing sugar, then the salted caramel flavouring. I'd add the icing sugar one or two tablespoons at a time when mixing so you can judge the texture you want. When it is light and fluffy, slightly firm in its consistency, you can then spread the frosting over the cake using a palette knife. Leave to chill in the fridge for 10 minutes.

If you don't want to add the flavour to the frosting, you can drizzle some caramel chocolate over the top, or mix icing sugar and salted caramel flavouring to a pouring consistency and drizzle this on top.

Oban Bay pontoons

Vanilla chai sponge cake

Recipe by Mikaela

CHAI SPICE MIX
4tsp ground cinnamon
2tsp ground ginger
2tsp mixed spice

SPONGE
290ml milk
2tsp chai mix
290g plain flour
2 1/4tsp baking powder
1/2tsp bicarbonate soda
4 tsp chai mix
1 1/4tsp salt
226g unsalted butter
360g caster sugar
3 whole eggs
112g sour cream
1tbsp vanilla essence

Combined all the spices for the Chai Spice Mix together and set aside.

Preheat the oven to 170C and line three 8-inch round cake tins and set aside.

Boil the milk and two teaspoons of the chai mix together, set aside and allow to cool to room temperature.

Mix all the dry ingredients together. Cream together the butter and sugar until light in colour. Whisk together the eggs, sour cream and vanilla essence.

Pour the egg mix into the creamed butter, followed by the dry mix, and lastly the cooled spiced milk (the mix will be thinner than a normal cake batter). Pour into the three ready lined cake tins and bake for 30–35 minutes until sponge is fully cooked and a skewer or thin knife blade comes out clean.

Turn out onto a wire rack and allow to cool completely before decorating.

Building & decorating
Use the Swiss meringue buttercream recipe (see page 25) to build and decorate the cake. Before building put some of the chai spice mix through the buttercream to flavour slightly.

Place your first sponge on a cake board or plate, and spread a nice thick layer of buttercream on top. Add the second sponge and do the same.
Once all three spongers are layered up coat the top and sides in more buttercream and decorate as you please.

Victoria sponge

One of our long-standing friends is Nick the Plumber. He took on his business next door to us about the same time we opened – right at the beginning of a recession (the very first hard seven years). Over the years he has been a reliable help in moments of plumbing crisis and we have shared emotional moans (me!) about being in business for yourself. We have supplied him with many bacon rolls over the years and, of course, cake. His favourite is Victoria sponge. In fact, I've made him so many over the years that perhaps we should call it Nick's Victoria!

225g margarine
225g caster sugar
225g self-raising flour
4 eggs
1tsp vanilla essence
1tbsp milk

FROSTING
125g salted butter, softened
125g cream cheese
500g icing sugar

Preheat oven at 180C/Gas 4. Grease two 8-inch Victoria sponge sandwich tins and line the bottoms with parchment paper.

Using a freestanding mixer place all the ingredients into the bowl and whisk on high speed until the mixture is light and fluffy – usually about one minute, no longer. Be careful not to over mix as this will cause the sponge to be heavy.

Divide the mixture into the cake tins and bake for 25–30 minutes, then leave to cool for a short while before turning out onto a wire rack to cool completely.

Once cool, sandwich the two cakes together with frosting or cream and jam of your choice, then lightly dust with icing sugar.

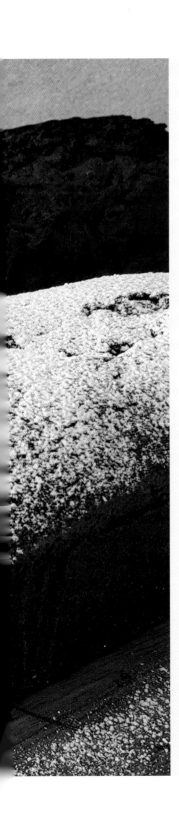

Loaves

Lemon & poppyseed drizzle loaf

This is a very popular cake and is lovely with a cup of tea. You can make it without the poppyseeds if you wish.

We had some tourists in on this one occasion and they loved the lemon drizzle loaf. They also liked our collection of teapots. So the day after they had visited the cafe, they came in again with a gift. They had been into one of the charity shops in Oban and had seen this novelty teapot and thought of us at Roxy's. We were taken aback as it was such a lovely gesture. The teapot still has pride of place in the cafe today.

225g margarine
175g caster sugar
Zest and juice of 3 small, or
two large, lemons
4 eggs
175g self-raising flour
50g ground almonds
1tbsp poppyseeds
Icing sugar

Preheat oven at 180C/Gas 4. Grease a 2lb loaf tin and line the bottom with baking parchment.

Using a freestanding mixer cream the margarine and caster sugar together until light and fluffy. Add the eggs and whisk for a few seconds, then add the sifted flour, poppyseeds and ground almonds, plus zest and two tablespoons of juice. Fold this in or mix on a slow speed. Don't worry about it curdling. Once incorporated, spoon the mixture into the baking tin.

Cook in the middle shelf of the oven for 45–50 minutes. To check if cooked, place sharp, thin knife in middle. If it comes out clean then it is ready. If not, return to the oven for five minutes.

Once the lemon cake is out of the oven, while it is still hot and in the tin, prick all over with a sharp knife. Heat the rest of the lemon juice with icing sugar and then pour the lemon syrup over the cake. Once the cake is cold, turn it out of the tin.

Make up some lemon icing by mixing cold lemon juice with the icing sugar. Make it much thicker than the syrup, then spread this over the cold loaf. The icing needs to be quite thick, then you can sprinkle a little zest over it if you wish.

Can be cut into 9 slices.

Cherry & banana loaf

170g butter or margarine
170g caster sugar
1tbsp grated orange zest
3 eggs
170g self-raising flour
1 banana
2tbsp orange juice
115g glacé cherries
1tbsp flaked almonds

Preheat oven at 180C/Gas 4. Grease a 2lb loaf tin and line the bottom with baking parchment.

Using a freestanding mixer cream the margarine and caster sugar together until light and fluffy. Add the grated orange zest. Gradually add the eggs, mixing in a little sifted flour after adding each egg until all the eggs are included, then lightly fold in the remaining sifted flour.

Mash the banana with the orange juice, adding this to the mixture, then add the cherries and stir lightly.

Spoon the mixture into the loaf tin and bake for 40–45 minutes. Check if it is cooked by piercing with a sharp knife, if it comes out clean you know it is ready.

Can be cut into 9 slices.

Raspberry & oatmeal loaf

We had some ladies from Edinburgh in Roxy's who asked to speak to me. They wanted to know how I made the cakes they were eating, so I explained and wrote down the recipes. We had a great chat and it was lovely to meet them. A few weeks passed and a recipe book arrived. Many women had got together, including the ladies that had come to the cafe that day, and had put together a book of various recipes – meals, puddings and cakes, including some of the recipes I had given them. The message with it said that if ever I published a book of recipes for Roxy's cakes, could I send them one. That was a dream back then, now it has become a reality!

115g margarine
115g caster sugar
115g self-raising flour, sifted
1/2tsp baking powder
60g oats
2 eggs
1 orange – 1 to 1.5tbsp juice
150g raspberries
Icing sugar

Preheat oven at 180C/Gas 4. Grease a 2lb loaf tin and line the bottom with baking parchment.

Using a freestanding mixer, cream butter, orange zest and caster sugar together until light and fluffy. Gradually add the eggs and mix well.

Add a little of the sifted flour and mix, then fold in the rest of the flour, plus the baking powder, then fold in the oats. Once the ingredients are completely incorporated, stir in the raspberries.

Pour the mixture into the loaf tin and bake for about an hour – check after 45 minutes by piercing with a sharp knife, if it comes out clean you know it is cooked.

Can be cut into 9 slices.

Fruit dumpling

This is a boiled fruit cake not a Cloutie Dumpling. It has a lovely texture and is quicker to make. I was given this recipe by my mother-in-law and I have adapted it to suit me.

FRUIT MIX
360g mixed fruit
115g caster sugar
225ml water
1tsp bicarbonate of soda
2tsps mixed spice
1/2tsp cinnamon
1/2tsp nutmeg

2 eggs
115g plain flour
115g self-raising flour

Preheat oven at 180C/Gas 4. Grease a 2lb loaf tin and line the bottom with baking parchment.

Put all the fruit mix ingredients into a large saucepan and bring to the boil, then lower the temperature to simmer, stirring occasionally for about 10 minutes. Take off the heat and leave to cool. This works if you want to leave it till the next day, just add a touch more water.

Add the eggs, plain flour and self-raising flour to the fruit and mix together well until everything is completely incorporated.

Pour the mixture into the loaf tin and bake for about an hour – check after 45 minutes by piercing with a sharp knife, if it comes out clean you know it is cooked.

Leave in tin until cold. Can be cut into 9 slices.

Gingerbread

225g self-raising flour
1tsp bicarbonate of soda
1tsp ginger
1tsp cinnamon
1tsp mixed spice
115g butter
115g treacle
115g golden syrup
115g dark sugar
275ml milk
1 egg

Preheat oven at 180C/Gas 4. Grease a 2lb loaf tin and line with baking parchment.

Place the flour, bicarbonate of soda, ginger, cinnamon, and mixed spice into a food processor with the butter and mix thoroughly.

Place the treacle and syrup in a saucepan and gently warm. Place the sugar and milk in another pan and gently warm until the sugar dissolves. Leave to cool.

Whisk the milk and egg into the cake mixture, then add the treacle and syrup mixture.

Pour into a loaf tin and bake in the middle shelf of the oven for 40–45 minutes. To check if cooked, place a sharp, thin knife in middle. If it comes out clean then it is ready. If not, return to the oven for five minutes.

Can be cut into 9 slices.

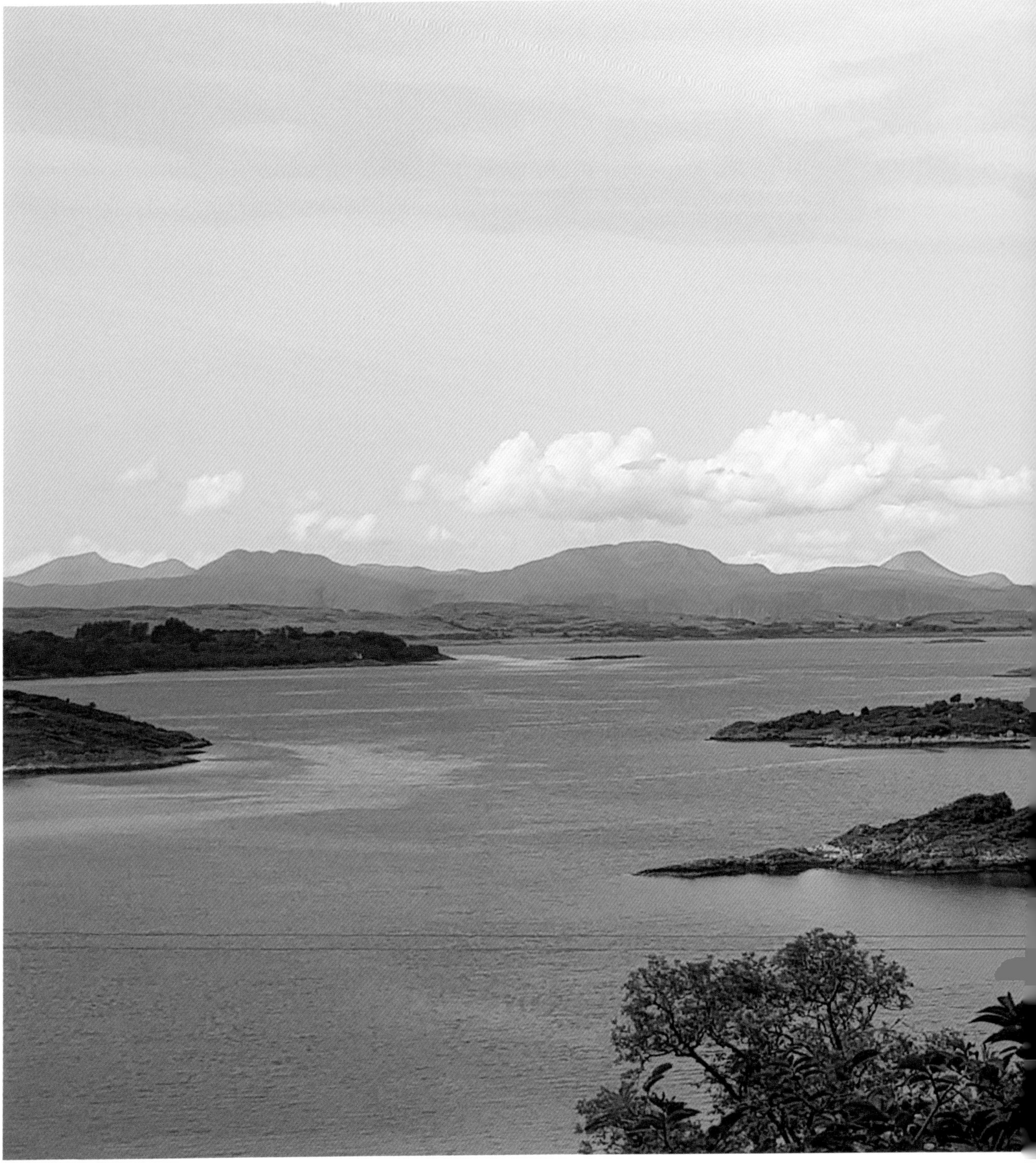

Loch Melfort from Kilchoan

Molly

Whenever I make scones I often think of a lady whose name was Molly. She was such a character and became part of Roxy's.

She was confident and proud and she would come in and say (in a posh accent): 'Scones and tea, please'.

Over time there was a table where she would always sit, and after a while she told us: 'This should be reserved for me and my scone and tea'. So when Thornton's sweet shop was still open in Oban and it was close to her birthday, we got a chocolate plaque made saying 'reserved for Molly' and we placed it on the table when we saw her arriving. Well, her face was priceless and we all laughed. She was overjoyed by this gesture.

After a few months – or was it years? – she developed a new phrase: 'where's the Shares man, I want my share?'. Molly meant my husband, Archie, who served with the army in the early days of Roxy's. So this new phrase could regularly be heard along with 'I'll have my usual scone and tea'. One day my husband was confronted by Molly in a lovely way. She said: 'Well, where's my share?' So Archie printed out a certificate for Molly. She was overjoyed by it. Over the years she became part of our Roxy's family.

Sadly, as she became frailer and her memory was not so good, we would watch out for her – the girls, Archie and myself. We'd make sure she had a bowl of soup and a sandwich – if we could coax her to eat. We had her daughter's telephone number and would keep her posted and updated on Molly's wellbeing, because this lady was very independent. Molly passed away but the memories she gave us at Roxy's will always stay with us.

So, the scones are for Molly.

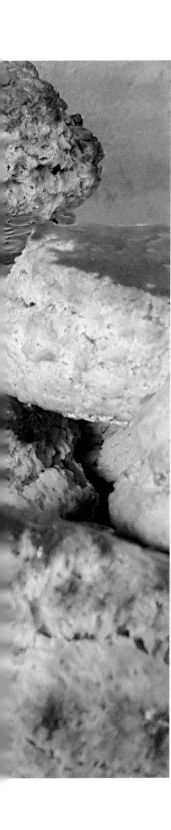

Scones

Scone mix

190g self-raising flour, sifted
260g plain flour
100g diced, cold butter
2tsp of baking powder
75g caster sugar
2 eggs
150–180ml milk or alternative,
such as soya or oat milk
Egg wash for glazing

TREACLE SCONES
1tbsp cinnamon
4tbsp treacle

APPLE & CINNAMON SCONES
2tbsp cinnamon
1 apple, grated or tinned apples

CHERRY & COCONUT SCONES
100g desiccated coconut
1tsp rosewater (or more to suit
your own taste)
Half a tub of glacé cherries
halved (more if you prefer)

LEMON & BLUEBERRY SCONES
Half a pack of blueberries
1 lemon zest and juice

Preheat oven at 150C (fan assisted)/Gas 4.

Place the flour, baking powder and the diced butter in a food processor and whizz until the mixture's texture resembles bread crumbs, then pour into a large mixing bowl. You can use the tips of your fingers to rub in the butter to achieve the same results.

Then add whichever flavour of ingredients your need to make your desired scones – see left. Set aside.

In a separate bowl whisk the eggs and add the milk together. Gradually add this liquid mixture to the scone mixture. Using a wooden spoon mix and bring the ingredients together.

Once everything starts sticking together, use one hand to gently form a ball, similar to when making bread. Add more of the egg and milk mixture as required – don't use all of the liquid unless you need it. You want an aerated, slightly sticky dough. You can also make more liquid if you need it, depending on what type of scone you are making.

Once the mixture has come together place onto a clean, lightly floured work surface and using your hands gently pat out and flatten into a circle, about an inch thick, lifting the edges of the dough while turning.

Use a serrated metal cutter to cut your scones – you want half the depth of the cutter for the thickness of your scones. Don't twist the cutter, just press straight down and then turn out onto a floured baking tray. Brush the tops of the scones with egg wash (see page 18).

Bake for 20–25 minutes or until golden brown and slightly firm to touch.

Makes 9 scones.

Cheese & spinach scones

This is how the cheese and spinach scone came about. I was making a muffin recipe and they were so messy I decided to try it as a scone. I used to make small amounts of them at first. Now I make much more and it's never enough. We have people who come in early to buy them or phone in orders. If I am out shopping I often get asked, 'Oh, I'm coming in on such and such a day, can you put some by for me please'. This also happens to the staff. Lol!

190g self-raising flour, sifted
260g plain flour
100g diced, cold butter
2tsp of baking powder
2 eggs
150–180ml milk or alternative, such as soya or oat milk
1/2tsp cayenne pepper (2x 1/4)
1/4 dry mustard
Good handful of spinach
Good handful of grated cheddar cheese
1/2 red onion, chopped
Egg wash for glazing

Preheat oven at 150C (fan assisted)/Gas 4.

Place the flour, baking powder and the diced butter in a food processor and whizz until the mixture's texture resembles bread crumbs, then pour into a large mixing bowl. You can use the tips of your fingers to rub in the butter to achieve the same results. Add the cayenne pepper, mustard, spinach, cheese and onion. Set aside.

In a separate bowl whisk the eggs and add the milk together. Gradually add this liquid to the scone mixture. Mix using a wooden spoon to bring the ingredients together. Once everything starts sticking together, use one hand to gently form a ball, similar to when making bread. Add more of the egg and milk mixture as required – don't use all of the liquid unless you need it. You want an aerated, slightly sticky dough. You can also make more liquid if you need it.

Once the mixture has come together place onto a clean, lightly floured work surface and gently pat out and flatten into a circle, about an inch thick, lifting the edges of the dough while turning.

Use a serrated metal cutter to cut your scones – you want half the depth of the cutter for the thickness of your scones. Don't twist the cutter, press straight down and then turn out onto a floured baking tray. Brush the tops of the scones with egg wash (see page 18).

Bake for 20–25 minutes or until golden brown and slightly firm to touch.

Anderson Banks, a legal firm in Oban, always place a weekly order with us on a Thursday morning – bacon and Lorn sausage rolls, and a sausage for Bramble the dog (above).

On one occasion we received a phonecall telling us we'd forgotten the sausage for the dog. Luckily the office is just across the road, so off one of the girls went with the said sausage. The relief on the staff's faces when she arrived… they said it is torture eating their Thursday treat without Bramble having hers. The dirty looks they would get would not be worth it!

Here are some other dogs that come to visit Roxy's.

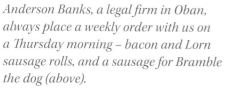

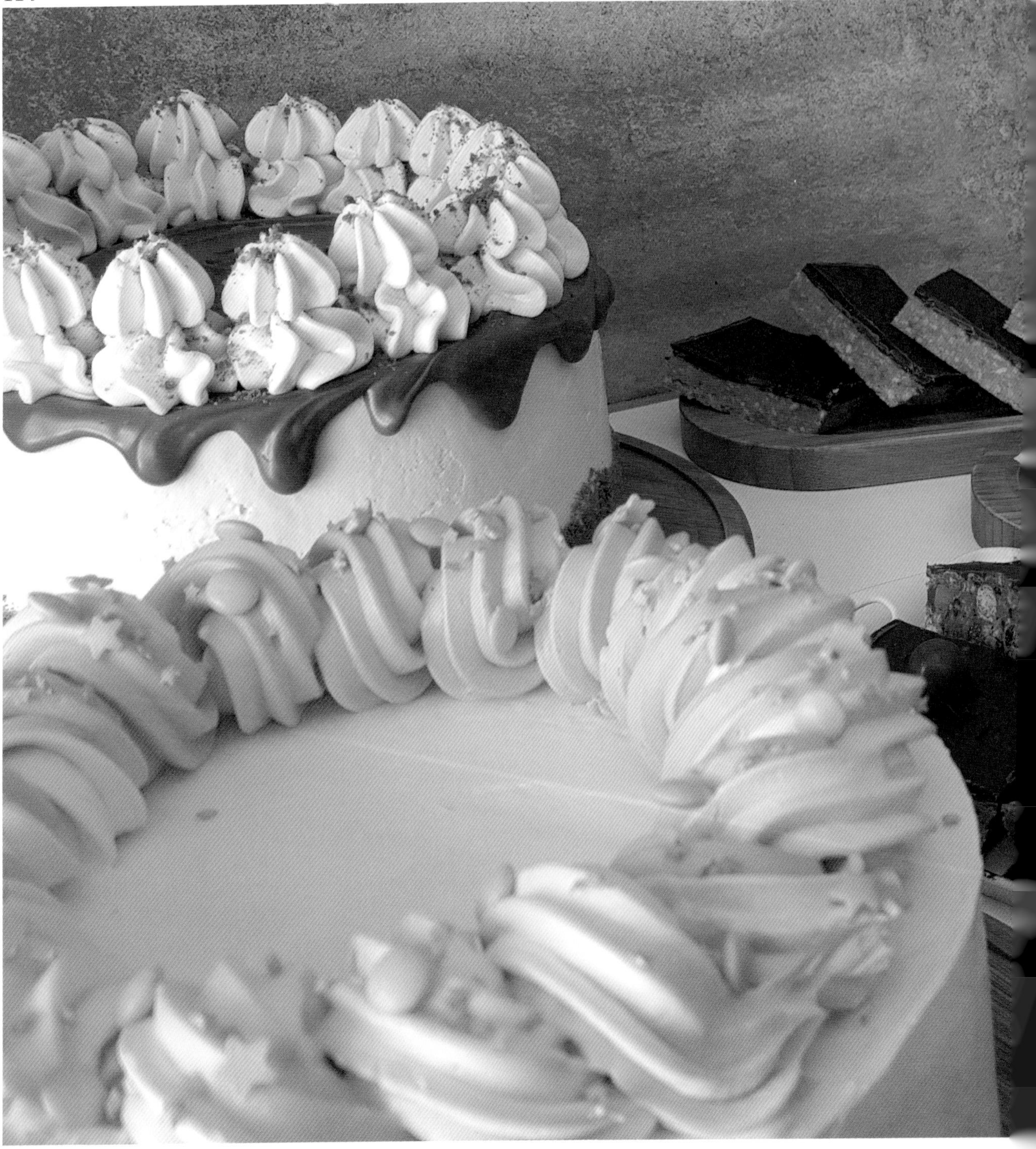

Holidays are for cake

It's amazing, it does not matter how many cakes you have in your notebook, and how many you make to put on your shelves/counter to sell, you always want to produce or invent more.

Whenever I go away I want to spend time in coffee shops and bakeries. I admit, if I was brave enough I'd ask if I could see where the people make their beautiful products.

When I was on holiday in Barcelona with my daughter and daughter-in-law, I insisted we popped into some of the bakeries that 'sold' me on their window displays. They would wait outside for me, wondering when I'd have enough of this fascination. I never have! Lol!

Biscuits
& other treats

Empire biscuits

In the early days of Roxy's my mother-in-law Marion used to help me bake. One of her recipes, the Empire Biscuits, were the best I've ever tasted. When she was unable to make them for me anymore, she passed on the recipe. 'So much flour, a little icing sugar and a block of butter, It's easy,' she said. But mine were just not turning out the same as hers, and after several attempts I decided to see how she measured the icing sugar. It was her aunt's old shell type silver spoon. 'Just one of those,' she said. Well, I'd taken my scales with me and let her put her spoonful onto the scales. Exactly 2.4oz – no more, no less. To this day that's the measurement we use and it comes out perfectly each time. There is a wonderful group of people from Glasgow who come into Roxy's every year and actually order six to eight of these to take away every time.

250g salted butter (softened)
2.4oz icing sugar
12oz plain flour

225g icing sugar to make your topping
Jam of your choice
Glacé cherries or sweet of your choice

Preheat oven at 180C/Gas 4.

Mix all the ingredients by hand into a pliable dough. Then, on a slightly floured surface, roll out the dough with a rolling pin to a 1/2 inch thickness (12mm). Then use a metal cutter – I use a serrated one – to cut your biscuits and place on a baking tray. Do not twist the cutter, just press straight down and then gently lift the biscuit dough onto the baking tray.

Bake for 12 minutes.

Once biscuits are cold sandwich two together with jam. Put a small amount of icing on the top, and then decorate with cherry or sweet of your choice.

You can vary the jam and topping – use lemon zest in the icing and sandwich together using lemon curd, for example.

Ginger & pear muffins

Recipe by Mikaela

MUFFIN MIX
195g butter
1tbsp treacle
135ml single cream
25g steam ginger in syrup
225g soft brown sugar
3 whole eggs
225g plain flour
2tsp ground ginger
1tsp ground cinnamon
2tsp baking powder
1/2tsp bicarbonate soda
1/2tsp salt
1 tinned pear halves
blueberries to decorate

BUTTER ICING
250g unsalted butter
100g cream cheese
300/400g icing sugar

Preheat your oven to 180C, then line your muffin tin with 10 tulip muffin cases and set aside.

Weigh out your stem ginger and finely dice, drain the tinned pears and roughly cut in to chunks.

In a heat-proof bowl, place in the butter, treacle, single cream, and diced stem ginger. Allow to melt over a saucepan of simmering water then remove from the heat and cool to room temperature.

Weigh out all the dry ingredients together. Cream the butter and sugar until light in colour. Pour the wet mix into the creamed butter, followed by the dry ingredients, mix until everything combined and smooth.

Pour enough batter into each muffin case to cover the bottom. Place 2/3 chunks of pear on top, then divide the rest of the batter between the muffin cases, pouring on top of the pear chunks, then place in the centre of the oven and bake for 30–35 minutes until the sponge is fully cooked and a skewer comes out clean. Place on to cooling rack and allow to cool completely.

Using a hand whisk, whisk the room temperature butter until soft and smooth then whisk in the cream cheese until smooth. Add the icing sugar, bit by bit, until combined to the desired constancy.

Place your butter cream in a piping bag with a piping nozzle, and pipe a nice big round bulb on top.

Once all the muffins are piped with buttercream decorate with some more pear chunks and some blueberries.

Jaffa muffins

Recipe by Mikaela

MUFFIN MIX
275g self-raising flour
3tbsp cocoa powder
1/2tsp salt
175g caster sugar
1tsp bicarbonate soda
300ml whole milk
150ml vegetable oil
2tbsp golden syrup
1tsp orange essence
1 orange zested

BUTTER ICING
250g unsalted butter
100g cream cheese
300/400g icing sugar
3tbsp cocoa powder
1 orange zest
50g marmalade

Preheat the oven to 180C and line your muffin tin with 10 tulip muffin cases.

Place all muffin mix ingredients (excluding the biscuits) into a mixing bowl and mix until well combined and smooth.

Spoon a large spoonful of the muffin mix into muffin case (enough to cover the base of the cases) and then place one whole Jaffa cake biscuit on top. Now divide the rest of the muffin mix between the cases to cover all the biscuits.

Bake for 25–30 minutes until sponge is fully cooked and skewer come out clean. Place on cooling rack and allow to completely cool.

Using a hand whisk, whisk the room temperature butter until soft and smooth, whisk in the cream cheese until smooth again and then add the icing sugar, bit by bit, until combined to the desired constancy. Now whisk in the cocoa powder, a spoonful at a time, and some orange zest.

Place your butter cream in a piping bag with a star nozzle, and pipe a circle around the edge of the muffin, leaving a gap in the middle. Once all the muffins are piped with buttercream place a teaspoon of marmalade in the centre of the buttercream where you have left a gap, and top with half a Jaffa cake biscuit.

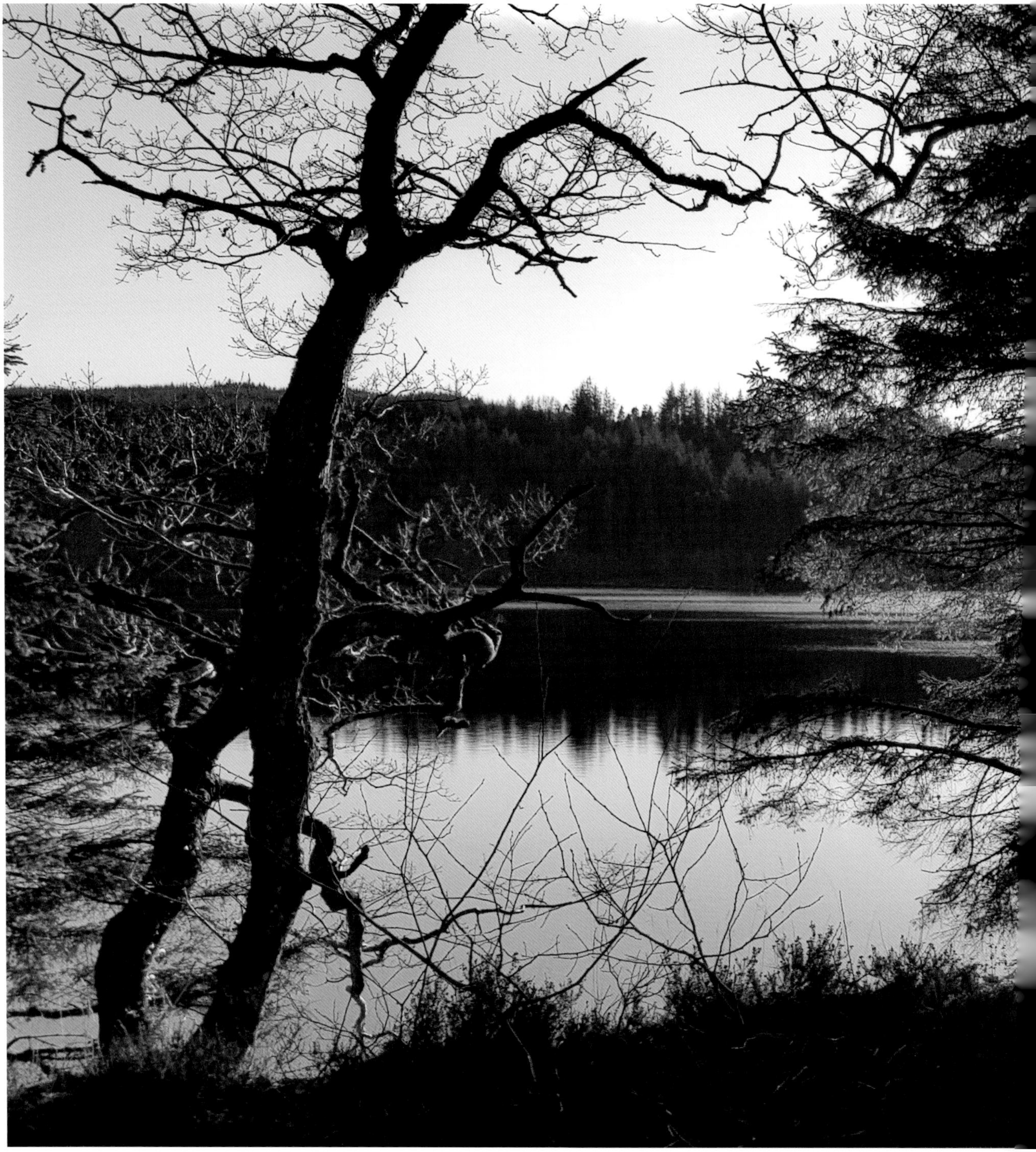

Loch Avich

Meringues

My mother-in-law gave me this recipe as her meringues were to die for. However, the first time I made them – she usually made them so I never bothered – I started off, as it seemed quite in the cafe, by putting the egg whites in the bowl and was just about to follow her instructions of gradually adding the sugar while whisking when my husband, who was cooking, started getting busy and needed my help. Well, a few heated words were said and I ended up putting all the caster sugar in at once. OMG! I didn't want to waste the ingredients, so I just put the freestanding mixer on meringue whisk for 10 minutes or until the mixture was firm. Lol! It got roughly spooned onto the baking tray and after one and a half hours, hey presto! They came out just the way I wanted – crunchy on the outside, soft on the inside. A success! From that moment on that was how I made them.

Makes 16 meringue portions

6 egg whites
340g caster sugar

Preheat oven to 110C/Gas 1. Grease two flat baking trays and line with baking parchment.

Place ingredients in a freestanding mixer – the bowl must be very clean and completely dry – and whisk on high speed for 10 minutes or until the mixture is very stiff.

Using a dessert spoon, place heaped spoonfuls of the mixture on your baking trays. The mixture should make 16 individual meringue portions.

Place on any shelf in the oven for 1 hour and 30 minutes.

Once cold, sandwich two meringue portions together with fresh cream, and decorate with a strawberry half.

Shortbread

There seems to be many variations and methods of making shortbread and a preferred taste. I love this one, however I judged a shortbread competition once and it is very competitive. Lol! I'm afraid to say I came away preferring mine.

Serves 12

340g plain flour
250g salted butter
115g caster sugar
115g cornflour

Preheat the oven at 180c/Gas 4. Grease an oblong baking tin and line the bottom with baking parchment.

Using a food processor whizz the butter, flour and caster sugar together until they resemble the texture of sand. Pour into the baking tin. Make sure the mixture is evenly spread across the tin and press down firmly. Bake for 25 minutes until light golden in colour.

When you take it out of the oven, cut the shortbread while still hot into 12 slices or however many you wish, then sprinkle with some caster sugar.

Leave until cool then take out of the tin.

Ferrero Roche chocolate millionaire

Recipe by Mikaela

SHORTBREAD BASE
250g unsalted butter
340g plain flour
115g caster sugar
1/2tsp salt

CARAMEL
See page 23

GANACHE
400g whole hazelnut milk chocolate
150g double cream
1tbsp unsalted butter

TOPPING
300g milk chocolate
8 Ferrero Roche

Preheat your oven to 180C and line a baking tray with baking parchment then set aside.

Using a food processor, blend together all the ingredients until you get a nice sand consistency. Pour the mixture into your ready-lined baking tray, make sure it is evenly poured in, right to the edges, but don't press down. Bake for 25–30 minutes or until a nice golden colour. Allow to cool completely before pouring the caramel on top.

Pour the caramel directly onto the cooled shortbread base while the caramel is still hot, and allow to set and cool completely.

Gently melt together the cream and chocolate over a bain marie or in a bowl above a saucepan of simmering water. Once melted stir in the butter in small chunks until combined. Pour on top of the caramel layer making sure to get an even layer with evenly dispersed nuts.

Allow to set in the fridge before finishing with the topping.

Gently melt the milk chocolate over a bain marie making sure not to over heat. While the chocolate is melting cut all the Ferrero Roche in half and set aside. Pour the melted chocolate on top of the ganache and spread evenly making sure to get into the corners. Place the Ferrero Roche halves on top (three x five in rows).

Allow to set completely before cutting into portions.

Oban Esplanade

Millionaire slice

BASE
340g plain flour
250g cold salted butter, diced
115g caster sugar

CARAMEL
See page 23

TOPPING
400g dark chocolate
200g milk chocolate
1/2tsp vegetable oil

Preheat the oven at 180c/Gas 4. Grease an oblong baking tin and line the bottom with baking parchment.

Using a food processor whizz the butter, flour and caster sugar together until they resemble the texture of sand. Pour into the baking tin. Make sure the base is evenly spread across the tin and press down firmly. Bake for 15–20 minutes or until lightly golden in colour.

While the base is cooling, make the caramel. Leave to cool then spread over your base and chill in the fridge.

While this is chilling, break up the chocolate and placed into a glass bowl over a saucepan of simmering water or a bain marie. If using a bowl and saucepan make sure the water does not boil over and get into the chocolate.

Once all the chocolate has melted, add the oil, which helps prevent the chocolate from cracking, and mix well. Once ready tip this over the caramel and spread evenly then chill in the fridge.

Cut into slices.

Viennese fingers

I don't make these often, but they are one of my favourites. On this particular day I'd made a batch and was feeling rather pleased with myself. It was a joy to see people enjoying them. However, to my horror, I was clearing a table where two young girls had been sitting and they had left behind two of the ends of the Viennese finger on their plates. These are the best bits! How could you eat the middle and not the best bit, which is the chocolate 'ends'? These beautiful biscuits and they hadn't eaten them. I must have moaned about it all day – terrible I know! I'm sure the staff were sick of hearing me harp on about it.

200g butter, softened
200g plain flour, sifted
50g icing sugar
1/2tsp baking powder
200g milk chocolate

FROSTING
Icing sugar
125g salted butter, softened
100g cream cheese

Preheat the oven at 180c/Gas 4. Lightly grease and flour two baking trays. You will need a piping bag and a medium star nozzle for this.

Cream together the butter and icing sugar in a large bowl. Add the flour and baking powder. Mix together until everything is incorporated and the mixture is light and fluffy.

Spoon the mixture into the piping bag and pipe out finger shapes about three inches long, spacing them well apart.

Bake for 10–15 minutes until pale golden brown. Take out of the oven and allow to cool. As these are cooling, melt the chocolate in a glass bowl over a pan of simmering water or a bain marie. Do not let the water touch the bowl.

Once the biscuits are cold, dip the ends in the melted chocolate, then sandwich two fingers together with some butter frosting.

To make the frosting, mix together the softened butter, cream cheese, and icing sugar until light and fluffy. If you start by making a small amount and gradually add more of the three main ingredients you can get the consistency you require – not too soft, but firm and light. Once done, put it in the fridge for 10 minutes.

Pecan & caramel slice

BASE
250g salted butter
340g plain flour
115g caster sugar

CARAMEL
See page 23

TOPPING
Half a packet of pecans – enough to scatter over your caramel.
100g dark chocolate
1tsp vegetable oil

Preheat the oven at 180c/Gas 4. Grease an oblong baking tin and line the bottom with baking parchment.

Using a food processor whizz the butter, flour and caster sugar together until they resemble the texture of sand. Pour into the baking tin. Make sure the base is evenly spread across the tin and press down firmly. Bake for 15–20 minutes or until lightly golden in colour.

While the base is cooling, make the caramel. Once made, leave to cool then spread over your base and chill in the fridge.

Place the pecans all over the caramel and then chill in the fridge for an hour.

After an hour, break up the dark chocolate and placed into a glass bowl over a saucepan of simmering water or in a bain marie. Make sure the water does not get into the chocolate. Once melted add the teaspoon of oil to the chocolate, mix well and then drizzle this mixture over the pecans, place back in the fridge and chill for another hour.

Cut into 12 slices.

Whoopies

For the filling, make up some cream cheese frosting (see the previous page) and use a jam of your choice. For the topping, make up icing and sprinkle with hundreds and thousands. I find I'm always left with one without a partner, so a tasty taster!

125g salted butter/margarine
200g caster sugar
1 large egg
1tsp vanilla essence
400g self-raising flour, sifted
150ml milk

FROSTING
Icing sugar
125g salted butter, softened
100g cream cheese

Preheat fan oven 180c/Gas 4. Lightly flour or line a baking tray with baking parchment.

Mix the butter/margarine and sugar in a freestanding mixer using the paddle attachment until light and fluffy, then add the egg and vanilla essence, the flour and the milk, and mix until everything is well incorporated. The mixture should be smooth and thick.

Using an ice cream scoop – I tend not to overfill it – place each scoop on a baking tray, making sure they are well spaced. I usually get three rows of three on each tray.

Place in the oven for 15 minutes or until a lightly golden colour. Turn out onto a wire rack to cool.

While the Whoopies are cooling, make the frosting. Mix together the softened butter, cream cheese, and icing sugar until light and fluffy. If you start by making a small amount and gradually add more of the three main ingredients you can get the consistency you require – not too soft, but firm and light. Place in the fridge for 10 minutes before using.

Once the Whoopies are cold, use a teaspoon of butter frosting on one flat side and a teaspoon of jam on the other and sandwich together and place in a paper muffin case to keep them steady. Top them with icing and some hundreds and thousands. It doesn't need to look uniform, they just taste so delicious.

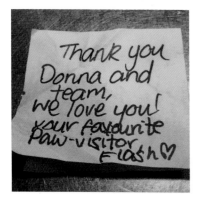

Thank you Donna and team, we love you! your favourite Paw-visitor Flash ♡

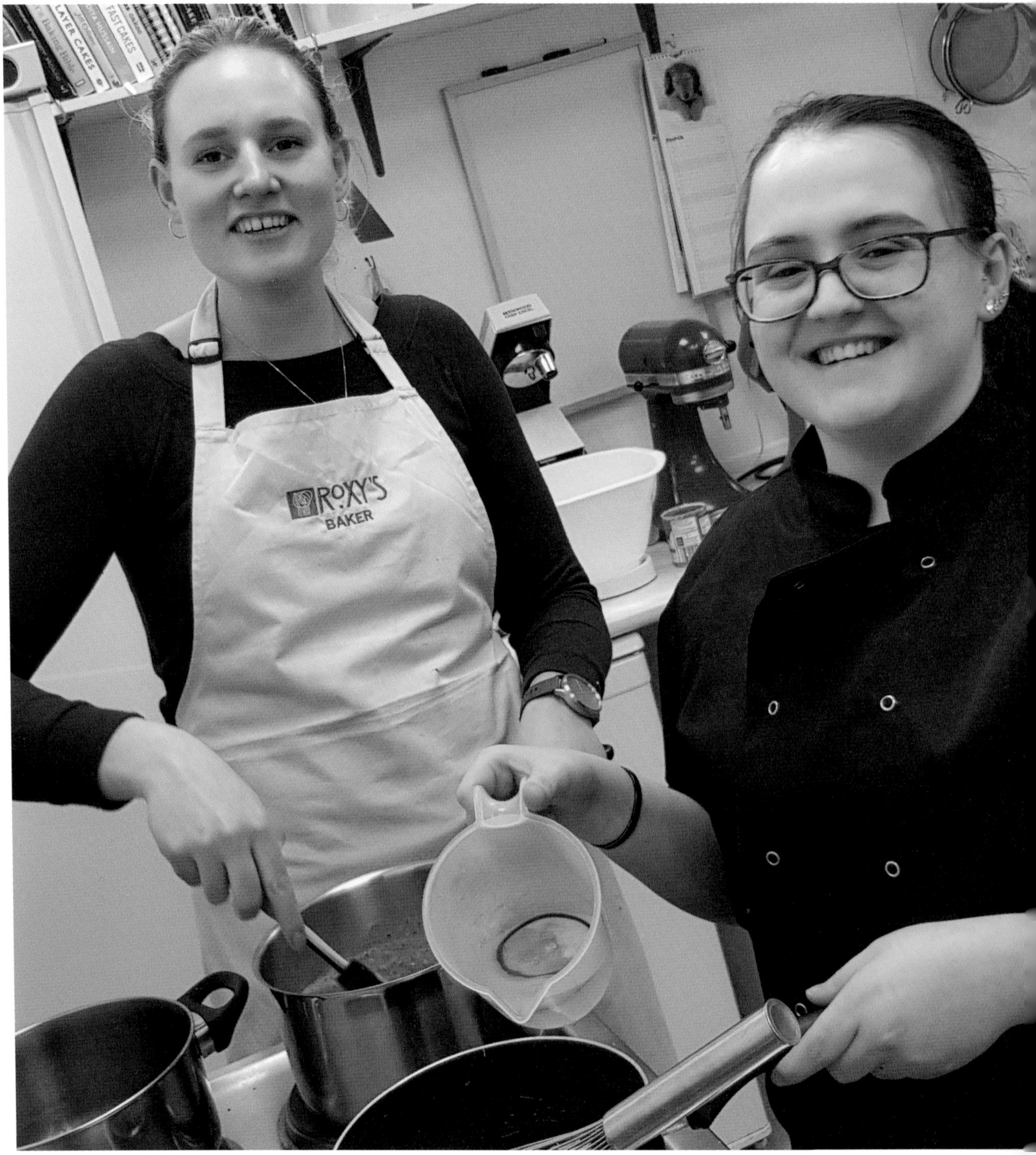
LAYER CAKES
FAST CAKES
ROXY'S
BAKER

Non-bake traybakes

Chocolate fudge

600g/1.5pkt Rich Tea biscuits
1 tin condensed milk
250g salted butter
400g milk chocolate

Grease an oblong baking tin and line the bottom with baking parchment.

Crush the biscuits or whizz them in a food processor until they resemble sand and then place them in a bowl.

Melt butter and stir in the condensed milk. Add this mixture to the biscuit crumbs and mix together until all the ingredients are completely incorporated. Spread the mixture into your baking tin and chill for half an hour.

For the chocolate topping, I use two large bars of Cadbury's chocolate broken up and placed into a glass bowl over a saucepan of hot water or bain marie. Make sure the water is simmering so that it does not boil over and get into the chocolate. Once melted, remove the bowl from the pan and leave to cool slightly.

Once the base is firm to the touch, pour the cooled, melted chocolate evenly over the top.

Place the traybake in the fridge to chill before cutting into slices.

Custard cream slice

One of my grandchildren, Ruaridh, calls this the rainbow cake because of the hundreds and thousands that are sprinkled over the top at the end.

4 packets custard creams or 2 double packets
1 tin condensed milk
250g salted butter (melted)
2 large or 4 small blocks of white chocolate
Hundreds and thousands sprinkles

Grease an oblong baking tin and line the bottom with baking parchment.

Whizz the biscuits in a food processor until they resemble sand and then place in a bowl.

Melt butter and stir in the condensed milk. Add this mixture to the biscuit crumbs and mix together until all the ingredients are completely incorporated. Spread the mixture into your baking tin and chill for half an hour.

While waiting for the base to firm, melt the chocolate in a glass bowl over a saucepan of hot water or in a bain marie. Make sure the water is simmering so that it does not boil over and get into the chocolate. Once melted, remove the bowl from the pan and leave to cool slightly before pouring over the base.

Once the traybake has cooled, sprinkle hundreds and thousands over the top.

Loch Tromlee

Gingernut fudge

Two and a half packets of
gingernut biscuits
250g salted butter, melted
1 tin condensed milk
400g white chocolate
100g dark chocolate

Grease an oblong baking tin and line the bottom with baking parchment.

Whizz the biscuits in a food processor and then place in a bowl.

Melt the butter and stir in the condensed milk. Add this mixture to the biscuit crumbs and mix together until all the ingredients are completely incorporated. If the mixture looks too wet, crush a few more biscuits and add to your mixture.

Spread the mixture evenly in your baking tin and press down firmly. Smooth the surface, then chill in the fridge for an hour.

Melt the white chocolate in a glass bowl over a saucepan of simmering water. Do not allow the water to boil over and get into the chocolate. Once melted, set aside and then melt the dark chocolate in a separate bowl over the simmering water.

Now, pour the white chocolate over the gingernut fudge, then drizzle the dark chocolate over in a pattern. Chill the traybake in the fridge overnight.

Jammie Dodger traybake

This is a must if you love Jammie Dodgers. It has been a difficult recipe to write down as I don't weigh and measure the ingredients – like so many, Lol!

600g white chocolate
200g salted butter
4 packets of Jammie Dodger biscuits

Grease an oblong baking tin and line the bottom with baking parchment.

Using a glass bowl over a saucepan of simmering hot water – making sure no water touches the bowl or steam travels up and around the bowl as this will affect the chocolate – break up and place 300g of chocolate and 200g of butter in the bowl. Stir this until all melted and well incorporated, then remove the bowl from the saucepan.

Now break up two packets of biscuits roughly (they will flatten down when you press them into the tin) and place into the mixture – always have one to nibble on!

Ensure the biscuits are well coated with the chocolate mixture then tip the whole lot into the baking tin. Spread over the whole tin and press down firmly. It may look like it is too thin but don't worry. Try to get it as smooth as possible and place in the fridge to set for one hour.

Now melt the remaining chocolate as before. Once the chocolate has melted, leave on the heat to stand for a while, just so the chocolate settles and becomes thicker again. You don't want it too runny.

Once ready, pour over the Jammie Dodger base evenly, then place the whole Jammie Dodgers from the remaining packets in a row on top of the chocolate while still wet. Put in the fridge to chill until next day.

Honeymoon slice

I would say this is the fastest-selling cake. As soon as we post on Facebook that I have made it, messages and requests to put some aside come flooding in!

Gavin, one of the plumbers next door, loves the honeymoon slice and will buy four slices at one time when it is on the counter. On one occasion the coffee machine was playing up. Without exception, this always happens on a busy Saturday. On this occasion we had the team of shinty lads in and a queue a mile long, which really didn't seem like an exaggeration at the time! Thankfully Gavin was in the queue and volunteered to sort it. Phew!

Luckily after undoing a few pipes and a bit of a mess under the counter, hooray, it was fixed – with extra, free cake and coffee for Gavin!

CARAMEL (See p23)

BASE (and little for topping)
200g dark chocolate
200g milk chocolate

TOPPING
400g white chocolate

MARS CRISPIE
3 Mars Bars
Butter
Golden Syrup
Rice Crispies

COCONUT BOUNTY
1 tin condensed milk
8oz desiccated coconut
4oz icing sugar
4oz butter

Grease an oblong baking tin and line the bottom with baking parchment.

Melt 200g of dark chocolate and 200g of milk chocolate in a glass bowl over a simmering saucepan of simmering water or in a bain marie. Make sure the water does not boil over and get into the chocolate.

Once melted, pour the mixed chocolate (leaving a little for the topping) into the baking tin and leave to chill in the fridge for half an hour.

Now make the Mars crispy. Using a non-stick saucepan, chop up the Mars Bars and put into the saucepan with the butter and Golden Syrup. Heat and stir with a wooden spoon until everything has melted.

Take off the heat and pour in the Rice Crispies. Stir thoroughly to ensure all the crispies are evenly coated – you may need more, or less, of the crispies. Turn out onto your chilled chocolate base.

Firmly spread Mars crispy mixture over the chilled chocolate then put back into the fridge to chill for

another half an hour. Now for the coconut bounty. In a bowl put the coconut, condensed milk, icing sugar and softened butter, mixing until everything is completely incorporated, then place on top of your Mars crispy. Chill again for another half an hour.

To make the caramel, put all the ingredients into a non-stick saucepan and heat gently until everything has melted. Bring the mixture almost to the boil, stirring continuously until the caramel starts to form.

Once you think it is thick enough, leave to cool slightly, then pour over the bounty mixture so that you now have four layers. Chill overnight.

For the final touch, melt the white chocolate as before. In a separate saucepan do the same with the remaining dark/milk chocolate mixture.

Take both off the heat – you need the chocolate to be spreadable and not too hot.

First pour and spread the white chocolate over the caramel, then drizzle the dark/milk chocolate over the top of the white chocolate. You can either do a feather design or a swirly design.

Chill again for an hour, then it is ready to slice, using a warm, sharp knife.

Author Alan Windram and illustrator Chloe Holwill-Hunter

Alan

Alan was a regular visitor to Roxy's, he was always pleasant and polite. He would order a slice of lemon fudge and a coffee. Sometimes we would get a message from his wife asking us to get him to buy two slices of the lemon fudge to take home. Clare and myself would often chuckle as he had already devoured one slice!

I can't quite remember how we found out that Alan, who is an author, had just won an award for one of his children's books, but we were so thrilled for him. The next time he visited he brought us in a copy signed for our children's book area that we had in the café, which was started by Meggie, one of Archie's aunties and was a great idea.

Alan and I had chatted about book writing and I mentioned that many a customer had asked me for a recipe and I would love to be able to write a book, however I felt it was beyond my capabilities.

A few weeks passed and Alan came in to chat with me in connection with writing a book – WOW! My reaction was shock, excitement and fear all rolled into one. I explained that I was slightly dyslexic. However Alan's wife Susan was there to design and produce the book for us and so another chapter began.

Lemon fudge

400g of digestive biscuits (Must be McVities)
200g desiccated coconut
250g melted butter
1 tin condensed milk
Zest of 3 lemons
Lemon juice
400g icing sugar

Grease an oblong baking tin and line the bottom with baking parchment.

Using a food processor whizz the digestive biscuits until resemble sand then tip them into a large bowl and add the coconut, melted butter and tin of condensed milk. Mix well with a wooden spoon until everything is incorporated.

Place the mixture into the baking tin. Ensure the mixture is spread evenly to a level consistency across the tin and chill in the fridge for an hour.

Grate the zest from the three lemons and squeeze the juice then set aside.

Place the lemon zest in a bowl and add the icing sugar. There is a balance here because you are looking for a thick but pliable mixture, enough to cover the biscuit base. So add the lemon juice a little bit at a time to the icing sugar and then add the zest until you are happy with the consistency. Spread over your biscuit base.

Place in the fridge overnight to chill.

Mars crispy

This Mars crispy recipe was given to me by Kerri MacCallum, many years ago. She use to waitress in Roxy's and help bake. There was never any measurements for this tray bake, just a chunk of butter, a glug of Golden Syrup, four Mars Bars and enough Rice Crispies to make the consistency required. All this was shown to me once, then it was all trial and error. This is the fun of baking!

400g milk chocolate, melted
4 large Mars Bars (5 if small), chopped
75g butter
1.5 cups of Golden Syrup (3 large glugs)
1 box of Rice Crispies (some of these will save for next batch)

Grease well an oblong baking tin.

In a large saucepan melt the butter, Golden Syrup and chopped Mars Bars. Keep stirring all the time as it may burn quickly. Start on a high temperature then reduce to half, making sure all the Mars Bars have melted and been incorporated.

Take off the heat and gradually stir in the Rice Crispies – I've never weighted them, I just measured by eye. You want enough crispies in the mixture to ensure all the crispies are completely covered. You also want the right amount of Rice Crispies in the mixture so that once hard it's not going to break your teeth!

Once this is done spread the mixture onto your well greased tin and ensure it goes right to the edges. Do not use greaseproof paper in the tin for this recipe.

Melt the milk chocolate in a glass bowl over a simmering saucepan of water. Make sure the water does not boil over and get into the chocolate. Once melted, pour the chocolate over the top and chill overnight in the fridge.

Cut into slices.

Mars Malteser

There is a couple who visit each year from Ireland – they sail their yacht across. They absolutely adore the Mars Malteser traybake. It's always a pleasure to welcome them back and to catch up. They usually give me notice as they like to take 8–10 slices away with them. They say they've tried many takes on this recipe elsewhere but it's never as good as Roxy's.

3–4 packets of chocolate chip cookies
4 Mars Bars
250g salted butter
1 tin condensed milk
1 small box of Maltesers
400g milk chocolate
1/2tsp of oil

Grease an oblong baking tin and line the bottom with baking parchment.

Using a large bowl, break up one packet of the cookies roughly and place in the bowl. Then, finely slice each Mars Bar and add to the bowl. Then whizz the remaining cookies down to crumbs in a food processor and add to the bowl. Add the box of Maltesers and mix everything together using a wooden spoon.

Melt the butter in the microwave – 20 or 30 seconds usually does it depending on the power of your microwave, but keep an eye on it – and pour over the biscuits, together with the tin of condensed milk. Mix everything thoroughly until it has all bound together.
You want the mixture to be tacky/moist but not too wet or dry as it needs to become firm enough to cut.

Place the mixture in the baking tin. Firmly flatten the mixture down and put in the fridge to chill.

While this is chilling, melt the milk chocolate in a glass bowl over a simmering saucepan of water. Make sure the water does not boil over and get into the chocolate. Once melted add the oil into the chocolate and mix well.

Pour over the biscuit mixture and leave to set overnight in the fridge.

Oban Bay from McCaig's Tower

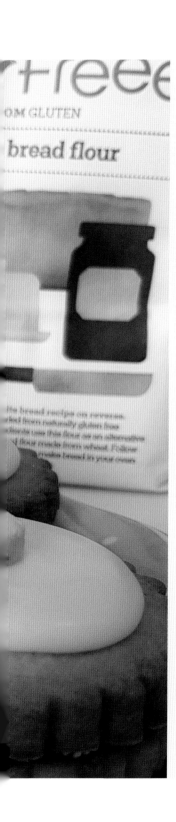

Gluten-free

Vanilla cupcakes

Thanks to Ellie for this recipe.

225g gluten-free flour
225g caster sugar
225g softened butter
1tsp vanilla extract
1tsp gluten-free baking powder
(or 2 parts of cream of tartar, 1
part bicarbonate of soda)
4 eggs
1/4tsp Xanthan gum (if available)

FROSTING
150g butter, softened
100g cream cheese
300g icing sugar (you can add
more if needed)

Preheat oven at 180C/Gas 4. Grease the muffin tin and place a paper cupcake case in each section.

Using a freestanding mixer place the butter, caster sugar, eggs, flour, and vanilla extract into the bowl and whisk vigorously for a minute until all the ingredients are incorporated. Your mixture should look light and fluffy. Don't over mix.

Spoon the mixture into each cupcake case, making sure you leave some room for the mixture to rise.

Place in the oven carefully and bake for 20–25 minutes or until lightly golden in colour but firm, and the mixture springs back when touched.

Make the frosting using a hand-held mixer. Place the butter, cream cheese and icing sugar in a bowl and whisk until light and firm, then place in a piping bag.

Once the cakes are completely cooled you can pipe on the topping using a spiral or rose petal nozzle on the piping bag and add some gluten-free sprinkles on top.

Brownies

Thanks to Ellie for this recipe.

150g gluten-free chocolate
100g butter
100g gluten-free flour
200g sugar
3 eggs
1tsp gluten-free baking powder
(or 2 parts of cream of tartar, 1
part bicarbonate of soda)

Preheat oven at 180C/Gas 4. Grease an oblong baking tin and line the bottom with baking parchment.

Break up the chocolate and place the pieces into a glass bowl over a pan of simmering water, making sure the water does not get into the chocolate, and melt.

Mix together the sugar, flour and eggs, then add the melted chocolate and butter and mix everything together.

Pour into your baking tin and bake for 20–25 minutes.

Cool on wire rack, then once cold cut into desired slices.

Scones

450g gluten-free flour
100g salted butter, cold and diced
2tsp of gluten-free baking powder
75g caster sugar (4tbsp)
1tsp Xanthan powder
2 eggs
150ml milk, more if needed
Egg wash for glazing (see p18)

Preheat the oven at 180C (fan-assisted)/Gas 4

Weigh out the dry ingredients and put into a food processor and whizz until the texture resembles bread crumbs, then tip into a large bowl.

Rub in the butter until you have the consistency of fine sand, then add the sugar using a wooden spoon. In a separate bowl whisk the eggs and milk together. Gradually mix in the liquid until you have a firm but slightly sticky dough. Do not use all the liquid unless you need it. You can also make more liquid if required.

Once the mixture start sticking together then use one hand to form a ball, similar to when making bread. Add more of the egg and milk mixture as required. You should have a sticky mixture which you then tip out onto a clean, lightly floured work surface and gently pat out and flatten into a circle about an inch thick using your hand, lifting the edges and turning.

Use a serrated cutter – I use a metal one as you get a cleaner cut – to cut your scones. Don't twist the cutter, just press straight down and then turn out onto a baking tray and brush to tops of the scones with egg wash.

Bake in the middle of the oven for 20 minutes or until golden brown and slightly firm to the touch.

Turn out onto a wire tray to cool.

Loch Etive from Glen Noe

Chocolate Swiss roll

175g dark chocolate
6 large eggs (separated)
175g caster sugar
2tbsp cocoa powder

FROSTING
150g butter, softened
100g cream cheese
300g icing sugar (you can add more if needed)
Raspberry jam

Preheat the oven at 180F/Gas 4. Grease your Swiss roll tin with butter and line with baking parchment, then butter the paper to make sure your sponge does not stick when baking.

Break up the chocolate and place the pieces into a glass bowl over a pan of simmering water, making sure the water does not touch the chocolate, and melt to a temp of 35C then set aside.

Separate the egg whites from the egg yolks in two separate bowls. Whisk the egg whites until they become stiff peaks and then set aside.

Whisk egg yolks with the caster sugar until light in colour. Fold the melted chocolate into the yolk mixture then gently fold in the egg whites, making sure not to knock out much air – you want a thick but light mixture. Lastly gently fold in the cocoa powder and pour the mixture into the lined Swiss roll tin.

Bake for 20–25 minutes.

Allow your sponge to cool completely in the tin and then place a clean, dry tea towel on your table top. Cover your tea towel with a piece of baking parchment and sprinkle a generous covering of cocoa powder on top.

Turn your sponge out on top of the dusted paper. Spread a thin layer of raspberry jam on your sponge, followed by a thin layer of vanilla buttercream. Slowly roll the sponge into the Swiss roll shape, wrap with the parchment and tea towel and place in the fridge to set.

Mini lemon meringue pies

350g gluten-free flour
100g butter
100g lard
1/2tsp salt
1 egg

FILLING
See page 24 for lemon curd

TOPPING
See page 126 for meringues

Preheat your oven at 180F/Gas 4. Grease a muffin tin.

Rub the butter, lard and flour together until it resembles the texture of sand, then add the egg yolk and mix well until it forms a dough-like ball. Wrap in cling film and leave for 15 minutes. I don't put it in the fridge.

Now roll out to your requirement. When rolling out pastry ensure it is a well-floured table and after each roll, lift the edges to stop the pastry contracting on itself. You can do this several times as long as you do not overwork the pastry – you will know if it is over worked if it becomes non-pliable and dense. Whether you are making mini tarts or one big tart, you want to roll your pastry to a 2cm thickness for both.

If making tarts, cut your circles using a plain metal cutter or a glass will do as long as the shape cut is large enough for what you require. Pop each pastry circle in the muffin tin and then prick the pastry dough all over, even the sides, with a fork.

Blind bake for about 10 minutes at 180c in a fan-assisted oven (see page 18 for blind baking)

Once cool, fill with lemon curd and top with individual spiral meringues.

Empire biscuits

2.4oz icing sugar
12oz g/f flour
250g butter
1tsp Xantum powder

Preheat oven at 180C/Gas 4.

Mix all the ingredients by hand into a pliable dough. Then, on a slightly floured surface, roll out the dough with a rolling pin to a 1/2 inch thickness (12mm). Then use a metal cutter – I use a serrated one – to cut your biscuits and place on a baking tray.

Bake for 12 minutes.

Once biscuits are cold sandwich two together with jam. Put a small amount of icing on the top, and then decorate with cherry or sweet of your choice.

You can vary the jam and topping – use lemon zest in the icing and sandwich together using lemon curd, for example.

Loch Tromlee

Anna and the shinty function

We were asked by the Camanachd shinty team if they could all come in for their breakfast before a big match. Anna was nominated and she volunteered to decorate the place with balloons and streamers etc to wish them good luck in the final match.

There was 47 of them for breakfast!

We sectioned off half the shop and organised a breakfast buffet area. On that particular morning we were also extremely busy with customers and had to explain to visiting tourists what was happening as the kitchen was very busy. However, there was quite a long wait and Anna did an excellent job of organising shinty sticks and feeding these hungry young men.

Savouries

Quiche

The great thing about quiches is you don't have to stick to the original recipe, you can invent your own. Maybe you have a few bits of vegetables lying about in your fridge, or tins of mixed beans in the cupboard (not baked beans!), or lentils, or just a selection of cheeses. All can be used with tasty results. And, depending on the size of your quiche dish, if you have pastry left over, you can make some lovely jam tarts for the children, or to bring back memories of your childhood. Using a shallow cup case tin or Yorkshire pudding tin as some call it, cut out circles using a pastry cutter and line the tin (no need to grease), then place a teaspoon of your favourite jam or curd in each and bake for 10–20 minutes. Just fantastic!

Shortcrust pastry (bought or see recipe on p16)
6–8 eggs depending on your need.
120ml double cream or 50ml milk
Salt and pepper to taste
2tsp mixed herbs

Filling of your choice

Grease a large flat baking tray or quiche dish and line with baking parchment. Shop bought pastry should have its own baking parchment so you will not need to line the tin separately. Roll out your pastry and lay in the baking tin. Prick the pastry all over with a fork and blind bake for 10–15 minutes. (See page 18 for tips on blind baking)

Once the pastry has cooked, place your filling in the pastry case. My filling is 1 onion fried, 1 pepper thinly sliced, 1 courgette, 1 large tomato sliced, half a block of Feta cheese, a handful of grated cheddar cheese.

Whisk together the eggs and cream – you do not have to add the cream or milk if you prefer not to. Pour over the filling.

Cook in oven 180c/Gas 4 for about 35 minutes. You know it is cooked if the centre of the quiche bounces back when gently pressed using your finger.

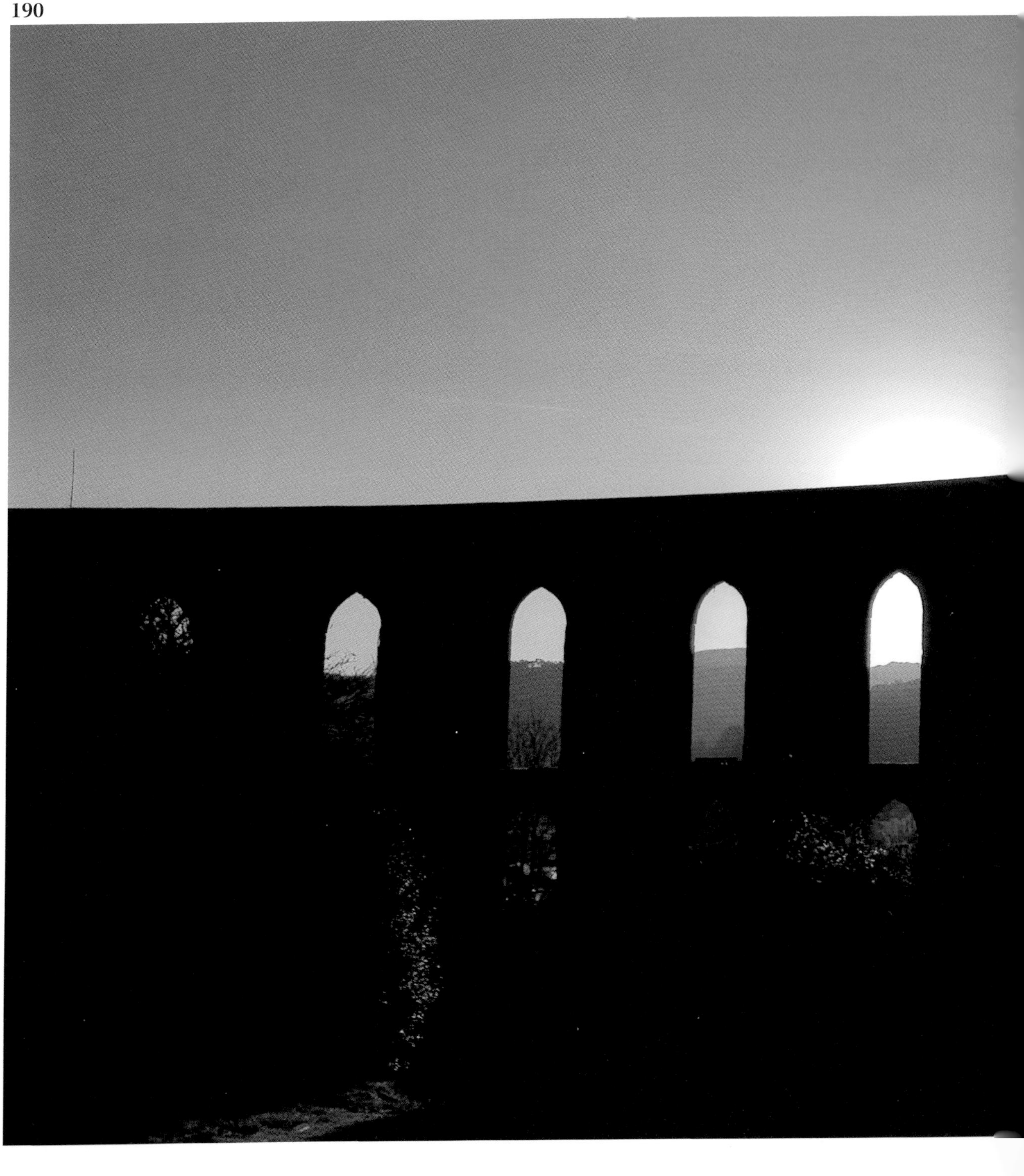

McCaig's Tower, Oban

Broccoli & mushroom quiche

Shortcrust pastry (bought or see
recipe on p16)
6–8 eggs
100ml double cream
Salt and pepper to taste
300g grated cheese
50g butter
1 onion sliced finely
2tsp mixed herbs
Handful of broccoli florets
1 clove of garlic sliced or crushed

Grease a large flat baking tray and line with baking parchment. Shop bought pastry should have its own baking parchment so you will not need to line the tin separately. Roll out your pastry and lay in the baking tin. Prick the pastry all over with a fork and blind bake for 10–15 minutes. (See page 18 for tips on blind baking)

In a wok or frying pan gently fry the onion and broccoli florets, herbs, salt and pepper to taste, and garlic in the butter.

Once gently sautéed and the onion and broccoli have softened spread evenly over your cooked pastry case.

In a separate bowl, whisk together the eggs, double cream, salt and pepper, and then pour over the vegetables and sprinkle on the grated cheese.

Bake in the oven at 180c for 30–40 minutes or until the centre bounces back or is firm to the touch.

Bacon, cheese & mushroom quiche

Shortcrust pastry (bought or see
recipe on p16)
6–8 eggs
100ml cream
1 pack bacon lardons (smoked)
1 onion, sliced finely
4 mushrooms
100g grated mature cheddar
Half a packet feta cheese
1 large beef tomato
Salt and pepper to taste
1tsp mixed herbs

Grease a large flat baking tray and line with baking parchment. Shop bought pastry should have its own baking parchment so you will not need to line the tin separately. Roll out your pastry and lay in the baking tin. Prick the pastry all over with a fork and blind bake for 10–15 minutes. (See page 18 for tips on blind baking)

These ingredients give the quiche a stronger flavour and texture as the lardons and two types of cheese are a lovely contrast, and the beef tomatoes are best if you can get them, as they tend to be juicier.

In a frying pan cook the lardons, onion and mushrooms with a good helping of pepper and a reasonable amount of salt and herbs.

Once these are gently cooked place in the cooked pastry case, then break up the feta over the ingredients, sprinkle the grated cheddar over this, then top with sliced beef tomato.

Cover everything with the beaten eggs mixture and bake in a pre-heated oven at 180c for 30–35 minutes until the centre of the quiche bounces back and feels firm to the touch.

Feta & spinach quiche

Shortcrust pastry (bought or see recipe on p16)
1 block of feta cheese
2 handfuls of spinach
6–8 eggs
100ml double cream
Salt and pepper to taste
1 garlic clove
1 large sweet pepper – yellow, red or orange – not green as your spinach is green.
2tsp mixed herbs

Grease a large flat baking tray and line with baking parchment. Shop bought pastry should have its own baking parchment so you will not need to line the tin separately. Roll out your pastry and lay in the baking tin. Prick the pastry all over with a fork and blind bake for 10–15 minutes. (See page 18 for tips on blind baking)

In a frying pan place your chopped onion, pepper and herbs and gently fry until tender.

Spread the mixture over your already cooked pastry case. Crumble the feta over the mixture, making sure it is evenly spread, then do the same with the spinach, tearing the leaves with your hands as this helps retain the peppery flavour of the spinach.

In a separate jug whisk together the eggs, cream, and add some salt and pepper to taste, and pour over the filling.

Bake in the oven at 180c for 30–35 minutes until it bounces back or is firm to the touch in the centre.

Goat's cheese & red onion chutney quiche

Shortcrust pastry (bought or see recipe on p16)
Red onion chutney (see recipe below for homemade, or use shop bought)
6–8 eggs
100ml double cream
Salt/pepper
1 packet of goat's cheese
1 handful of spinach (uncooked)
1tsp mixed herbs

Red Onion Chutney
4 red onions chopped finely
50g caster sugar
50ml red wine vinegar
A glug (1tbsp) Golden Syrup

Grease a large flat baking tray and line with baking parchment. Shop bought pastry should have its own baking parchment so you will not need to line the tin separately. Roll out your pastry and lay in the baking tin. Prick the pastry all over with a fork and blind bake for 10–15 minutes. (See page 18 for tips on blind baking)

To make the red onion chutney, put the red onions and sugar in a wok or deep frying pan and place on a medium heat and cover with a large lid. Cook until the onions are tender, then pour in the red wine vinegar and continue to cook uncovered until the liquid has reduced and is sticky – about 10 more minutes – then add the Golden Syrup and mix well. Leave to cool.

Once you have made the chutney and your pastry case, whisk up the eggs and cream and add the seasoning (salt, pepper, mixed herbs).

Spread a thin layer of the red onion chutney on to the pastry, then crumble the goat's cheese on top, rip up the spinach and add this, then pour the egg mixture in. If you need more to fill the pastry case just whisk up a couple of eggs and cream and top up.

Pop in the oven at 180c for 35–45 minutes. Check if it is ready at 35 minutes – the quiche should be firm to touch if ready.

Pasties

Shortcrust pastry (bought or see recipe on p16)
1lb lean mince beef steak
1 large onion, diced
1 potato cut into strips
Half a small swede/turnip, dice in thin strips
1/2tsp nutmeg
1tsp salt
1.5tsp ground black pepper
1 beef stock cube
1 egg for egg wash (see p18)

Fry the onion and mince in the butter and add the salt, pepper, nutmeg and crumbled beef stock cube. Once the mince has started to look cooked, add the swede/turnip and potato. Simmer on a low heat until everything is cooked. Leave to cool.

Roll out your shortcrust pastry to 2cm thick and cut circles. I use a small saucer.

With a pastry brush, paint egg wash around the edges of the pastry circles and put a couple of dessert spoonfuls of your meat filling in the middle, then gather the edges together and crimp the pastry together over the filling. A fork is an ideal tool for pressing down on the edges to seal and crimp them together.

Glaze the pastry with the egg wash and place on a flat baking tray. Continue to do this until all your ingredients are used up.

Bake at 180c for 20–25 minutes, until golden in colour. Cool on a wire rack. Enjoy hot or cold.

A slice of kindness

Ivor comes to Roxy's once a week on the bus from Kilmore, a small village just outside Oban. He is a quiet man, very polite and he always gets a bacon roll to take away.

Over the years, at Christmas time, he has always given the staff money or boxes of chocolates, and it has always been so appreciated. We often wondered what we could do for him.

Ivor was in just before the first lockdown happened in March 2020. It was the Thursday, his day for coming in, and he was very upset and concerned about how he would get his medication. So we went the next day and got it for him, and dropped it off with him. It was the least we could do after all the years he had been so generous to the staff at Roxy's.

Bluebell wood, Loch Awe

Chicken & mushroom pie

1 LARGE PIE OR 4–5 SMALL

Hot water paste pie pastry (see recipe on p17)
2 chicken breasts diced
6 mushrooms diced
1 leek sliced
1 clove of garlic crushed or 1/2tsp of garlic paste
50g of butter
Oil (veg or olive)
128g of plain flour
Salt and pepper to taste
Paprika or chicken seasoning
English or Dijon mustard
500mls of milk

To make a roux, put 50g of butter into a small saucepan and add the flour gradually, mixing vigorously (using a hand whisk or wooden spoon). When it forms a small ball-like lump, gradually add the milk, a little at a time. This may look like it will go lumpy on you, but keep mixing, beating it long enough, adding more milk until it has a smooth consistency. Add the mustard, salt and pepper, mixing all the time. Once you are happy with your roux, set aside.

In a frying pan, pour a little oil and gently fry the leeks, chicken, and mushrooms. Add a little salt and pepper, along with the chicken seasoning or paprika and the garlic. Cook on a low heat and cover until the chicken is thoroughly cooked, then set aside.

Using the hot water pastry recipe, grease and flour your small pie dishes/ large pie dish. Line the dish/es with the pastry and cut off any excess. Make sure you cut the lids for your pies as well and set them aside. Put the uncooked pie cases in the fridge for 30 minutes.

While the pastry is resting in the fridge, combine the chicken mixture with the roux, mixing well until everything is incorporated. If you feel your mixture is too thick, add a tiny bit more milk.

Once the pastry has rested for the required time, pour the mixture into your dishes, and using an egg wash (see page 18) seal the lids to the pies and pierce a hole in the middle of the pie lid with a knife, then brush the egg wash over the lid.

Bake for 20–30 minutes at 180c (fan assisted oven). Check after 20 minutes to see how they are goldening up.

Steak pie

1 LARGE PIE OR 4–5 SMALL

Hot water paste pie pastry (see
recipe on p17)
1kg of good quality steak
1 large onion
1 beef cube
1 bay leaf
Salt and pepper to taste
1/2tsp nutmeg
Water to cover meat

Fry off the steak and onion in a large pot with a little oil and seasoning, then cover with water and put in a beef stock cube.

Stir until the cube dissolves then add the bay leaf and nutmeg.

Simmer until tender (about three hours). Add more seasoning depending on taste. Once cooked, set aside.

Using the hot water pastry recipe (see page 17), grease and flour your small pie dishes/ large pie dish. Line the dish/es with the pastry and cut off the excess pastry. Make sure you cut the lids as well and set them aside. Put the uncooked pie cases in the fridge for 30 minutes.

Once the pastry has rested for the required time, pour the mixture into your dishes, and using an egg wash (see page 18) seal the lids to the pies and pierce a hole in the middle of the pie lid with a knife, then brush the egg wash over the lid.

Bake for 20–30 minutes at 180c (fan assisted oven). Check after 20 minutes to see how they are goldening up.

Barguillean's 'Angus Garden'

Sausage rolls

Shortcrust pastry (See recipe
p16)
Good quality sausage meat (we
use our local butchers, Jacksons,
Oban)
Salt and pepper to taste
Fresh parsley
1 egg for egg wash

In a bowl, place 1lb of sausage meat, salt and pepper to taste, and freshly chopped parsley.

Mix all the ingredients together and place in a piping bag. I don't use a nozzle. I then pipe out the sausage meat in a line on the centre of the pastry.

Using an egg wash (see page 18), wet one side of the pastry and cover over the sausage meat in a roll type fashion. Using a fork, press down the edge to keep the meat in. You can gently score the top of the sausage roll, then brush all over with more egg wash.

Slice into your desired length before baking.

Bake on a lightly floured tray for 15 to 20 minutes at 180/Gas 4.

The Elf Story

One year we hid an elf in the cafe and posted it on our Facebook page in the run-up to Christmas, so when children came in they had to spot where he was.

The staff had a lot of fun with this, from kitchen to front of house. All except Liam our chef, that was. Liam was petrified of him and the girls found places to hide the elf so that when Liam opened a cupboard, for example, the elf would jump out at him. This, I am ashamed to say, was highly amusing and gave the girls lots of laughs.

One year, one of our staff member's partner got his own elf and froze it in a block of ice and left us a ransom note saying it had been stolen! It turned up on the backdoor step one morning...it took a while for him to defrost.

Christmas mince pies

Serves 12

PASTRY
100g butter
100g lard
350g plain flour
Pinch of salt
115g caster sugar
1 orange zest
1tsp nutmeg
1tbsp orange juice

FILLING
Jar of mincemeat
170g currants
170g raisins
115g candied peel
1tbsp mixed spice
1tbsp cinnamon
2tsp nutmeg
200ml brandy or Amaretto
Rest of orange juice

1 egg for egg wash

Preheat the oven at 180c/ Gas 4.

Put all the dry ingredients for the pastry in a food processor whizz them until they resemble fine sand. Tip out into a large bowl then add all the orange zest to the mixture and mix well.

Make a deep indent, like a well, in the centre of the the mixture then add one egg and a dash of very cold water. Quickly mix together with one hand to form a dough-like mixture, bringing it into a ball. You may need a little more water as you are doing this but be careful not to add too much or it will make the dough sticky. If this happens you can add a little more flour.

Once the pastry is firm and smooth leave to rest at room temperature for five to 10 minutes.

You can either prepare the fruit filling on the day or a couple of days before hand.

Empty a jar of regular mincemeat (the fruit type) into a tub with a lid then add all the other fruits, spices and liquid. Stir and then leave.

Once your pastry has rested roll out on a floured board to about 2cm thick. Using a large serrated cutter cut out the pastry and place a pastry circle in each muffin tin that you have greased and floured.

Spoon the fruit mixture in – not too much as you don't want it overflowing. I then use a star-shaped cutter to cut the remaining pastry, popping a star on top of each pie. Using an egg wash (see page 18), brush the top of the pies and pop them in the oven for 15–20 minutes, until lightly golden brown. If you have extra pastry make a second batch when your first lot come out of the oven.

Once baked, take out of the oven and leave to cool for a few minutes then gently ease them out and don't worry if they break, these are for you to test first! Once cooled dust the top with icing sugar.

Lochawe near Taynuilt

Archie's bread mix

This recipe is for a basic white loaf.

1/2tsp caster sugar
290mls warm milk
450g strong bread flour
2tsp sea salt
2 eggs (1 egg for glazing)
7g dried yeast

Pre-heated the oven at 180c.

In a freestanding mixer, using the paddle attachment, place the flour and salt into the bowl. Mix the yeast and sugar in a jug containing the warm milk. Stir and wait a few seconds, then pour half of it into the flour, then beat in the egg to the remaining milk and add to the flour. Mix everything together on a medium speed for 10 minutes until the dough comes together.

Rest the dough in the bowl for 10 minutes then turn it out onto a lightly floured surface and knead until the dough feels smooth. Then shape it into a ball and cover with greased clingfilm and leave to rise in a warm place for an hour.

Once it has doubled in size, gently knock it back on a slightly floured surface for one minute. To knock back dough, push your fist into the centre of the dough and watch it deflate. Pull and stretch the dough a few times to remove any large air bubbles. This will also help develop the texture and flavour of the bread.

Shape it so you can either put into a greased and floured 2lb loaf tin or make your owned shape. If you are making your own shape you will need a flat baking tray that has been greased and floured to lay the dough on. Leave it to rise again for half an hour.

Once it has risen again, glaze with egg wash (see page 18). You can slice the top with a sharp knife to make a pattern if you wish.

Bake the loaf in the centre of the oven for 30–35 minutes or until golden and firm. The baked bread should sound hollow when you turn it out and tap the bottom of it.

Scotch rolls

500g strong flour
7g yeast
2tsp salt
1tsp sugar
100ml milk and 200ml warm
water combined
3tbsp oil
1 handful porridge oats

Pre-heat the oven at 180c

Combine flour, yeast, sugar, and salt, then add the milk and warm water. Mix well for 10 minutes. I find using a dough hook on your mixer is best. Remove the hook but leave the dough in the bowl to rest for 10 minutes.

Knead the dough with your hands for another 10 minutes until smooth and pliable. Cut the dough into sections, say six to eight pieces, and mould into round balls and place on a floured baking tray. Cover with slightly greased clingfilm – or for crisper rolls leave uncovered – and leave to rise for an hour in a warm place.

Once ready to be put in the oven, brush the tops of the rolls with milk and sprinkle some porridge oats on top and sea salt if desired.

Bake in the oven for 20 minutes until golden in colour. Remove and cool, or eat warm with melted butter. Yummy!

Soda bread

This recipe reminds me of my dad, who was Irish. It brings back many fond memories. In my home when I was a child, there was always bread and cakes being made. In those days the airing cupboard (a warm cupboard where the water heater was stored) was the best place to let the bread rise. I like to eat it while it's still warm with lots of butter, especially to accompany a bowl of stew or soup.

450g strong white flour
1tsp salt (I use sea salt)
1tsp bicarbonate of soda
150ml full fat milk
150ml plain natural yoghurt
5–6tbsp water

Pre-heat the oven at 180c

Put the flour, bicarbonate of soda and salt into a large bowl and mix together. In a separate jug mix the milk and yoghurt, then pour this liquid into the dry ingredients. Bring all the ingredients together using your hand. You may need to use the water at this point, but add it a tablespoon at a time. You don't want your mixture sticky.

Once you have a soft dough, turn it out onto a floured surface and shape it into a round size about 7 inches/18cm in diameter, then place on a slightly floured baking tray, and using a sharp knife, cut a cross on the top.

Bake in an oven for about 30 minutes, then turn the soda bread upside down and bake for a further 10 minutes.

Loch Etive

Index

Index